THE
FIELD&
STREAM
HUNTING OPTICS
H A N D B O O K

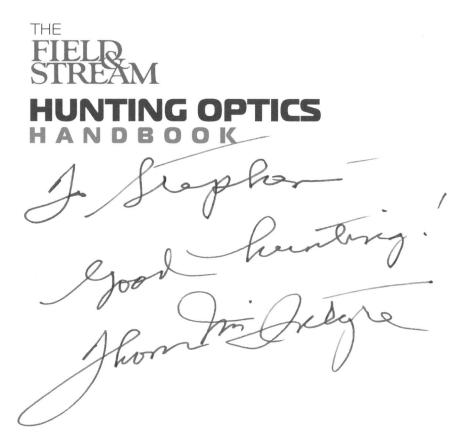

To Stephen —
Good hunting!
Thom McIntyre

THE
FIELD& STREAM

HUNTING OPTICS
H A N D B O O K

AN EXPERT'S GUIDE TO RIFLESCOPES, BINOCULARS,
SPOTTING SCOPES, AND RANGEFINDERS

THOMAS M^cINTYRE

 The Lyons Press
Guilford, Connecticut
An imprint of The Globe Pequot Press

To buy books in quantity for corporate use
or incentives, call **(800) 962–0973**
or e-mail **premiums@GlobePequot.com.**

The Lyons Press is an imprint of The Globe Pequot Press.

Illustrations © 2008 Andrew Warrington

Text Design by Mimi LaPoint

Library of Congress Cataloging-in-Publication Data is available on file.

ISBN 978-1-59921-044-5

Printed in the United States of America

10 9 8 7 6 5 4 3 2 1

The Aten
The ancient Egyptian name for the disk of the sun,
the sun the source of light, light the origin of vision,
vision the basis for optics.

CONTENTS

INTRODUCTION

Sight is the hunter's truest weapon and his most dramatic sense. Both hearing and touch are vital to the hunter, and even his sense of smell, perhaps not as acute as it once was when humans daily depended upon it for their survival, should not be discounted. But it's sight that comes to the fore in the most crucial moments of the hunt: tracking and sighting the quarry, keeping it in view, and using the information provided by sight to perform the complex course of mental and physical actions involved in aiming and firing a rifle, shotgun, or bow.

Many other animals are thought to have far greater visual acuity than humans, animals such as birds of prey and even the horse (the eye of the mule allows it to see all four of its feet at the same time). The human eye, though, is not to be discounted, being the product of hundreds of millions of years of evolution.

Yet as remarkable an instrument as the human eye is, it is not perfect, and can benefit from artificial aid. Humans have almost always been seeking ways to enhance their vision; but only in approximately the last five hundred years has the application of physics, math, chemistry, design, experimentation, and artisanship permitted serious advances to be made in the vision that is available to the naked eye.

Hunters have well understood the advantages afforded them by augmenting their vision. Even something as elementary as iron sights was a significant innovation. Today the options in vision aids, or optics (a word that shall be discussed further), for hunting are vast. What hunters need in order to weed through the bewildering array of riflescopes, binoculars, spotting scopes, rangefinders, shooting glasses, ad infinitum, though, is not a list of recommended brand names to purchase: The leap-frogging technology of optics makes shopping guides like that almost instantly obsolete.

What the hunter needs is guidance on the basic rules for what comprises quality optical instruments, and the proper care and use of them. Those critical aspects of optics always remain steady, and are what this book will endeavor to examine and explain, in the hope that an understanding of those aspects will help hunters improve their ability to select and use such implements, and increase their enjoyment of them in the field.

The author hopes that this book will fill the role of a teaching aid, rather than a buyer's guide. Think of it as a field guide to hunting optics. To such an end it seems necessary to begin with some of the most basic aspects of optics and build on them. If the points raised, the theories expressed, the historical record presented, and the technical information given seem superfluous at the time, it is the author's aspiration that by the end of the book the material it contains will have conspired to turn the reader into not just a knowledgeable consumer of optics but into someone with a clearer understanding of the optical process and the devices which he can use to enrich his appreciation of the visual world around him, and perhaps make him a better hunter in the bargain.

VISION   1

Optical instruments are made no finer than the human eye. To be admired as a piece of quality workmanship, the human eye is also the human's most essential survival tool. As such, it needs to be maintained, nourished, exercised, protected, and on occasion corrected.

To call the eye the most essential survival tool is to acknowledge the centrality of eye-hand coordination in the existence of humans and indeed, all primates in general. From the aspect of hunting, consider that classic scene in Stanley Kubrick's *2001: A Space Odyssey* in which the poor, put-upon *Australopithecine,* having received his inspiration from the mysterious black monolith, curiously hefts a desiccated femur and discovers it can be wielded rather nicely as a lethal weapon. Striking a herbivore's skull cleanly and fatally with a bone club may not seem like an overly elaborate example of tandem effort of vision and motor function, but try driving a nail straight in with a single hammer blow, and you gain a certain appreciation of the complexity of the task.

A mortal spear thrust requires a similar successful linkage of cortexes, and then there is the far more sophisticated procedure of delivering force at a distance, such as from a thrown rock or hunting stick, like a boomerang or a hurled javelin. Throwing at a target is different from "aiming" at one. There is no sight alignment involved, other than the thrower visualizing where he wants the projectile to go. The process is the same as pointing at an object with a finger. In the King James version of the Bible, David "put his hand in his bag, and took thence a stone, and slang *it*," the rock smiting Goliath in the center of his forehead and sinking into it. What David slang with would have been the aptly named "shepherd's sling," which would have consisted of a leather pouch attached to two long strings of woven animal hair. With a stone, often the size of a cue ball, in the pouch, the sling was spun at the thrower's side; at the bottom of the circle, one of the strings was released, and the stone would fly underhand from the thrower to the target. Such slings could send out their stones at velocities of 60 miles per hour and reach distances of up to a quarter-mile. In warfare, slung shots could strike specific spots on an enemy's face or body, all without the thrower's aiming because at no time would his eye be on the sling or the shot but rather exclusively on his target.

Archers who hunt with "bare" bows, i.e., without sight pins or other aiming devices, recognize this technique as "instinctive shooting." Again, it is a matter of the hand, the one holding the bow, pointing to where the eye is looking. An instinctive archer never "sees" the arrow, the string, or even the sight window on the bow but rather sees past all of those to his target. *Proficient* instinctive shooting is the product of repetitive practice at assorted yardages until the archer has a natural feel for where the arrow should go. How effective can instinctive shooting be?

Think of the centerfielder who can throw a baseball hundreds of feet into a catcher's mitt at home plate. Now add the mechanical advantage of a bow. Obviously, eye-hand coordination, married to a throwing device such as a bow, makes for the possibility of striking an object accurately at considerable range.

A critical factor in the eye-hand coordination that goes into the instinctive use of a sling, bow, a spear thrower like the ones known by the Meso-American Indian Nahuatl word *atlatl,* and even to some extent a shotgun, is the determination of the thrower's "master eye." We all know whether we are right- or left-handed, ambidextrous, or in some cases mixed-handed (which is a preference for using one hand in one type of work, such as fine-motor tasks, and the other hand in a different type of work). What we sometimes never realize, though, is that most of us have a dominant right or left eye. Generally, our dominant eye aligns with our dominant hand, but there are some people who have cross-dominance. This is what is also known as "mixed laterality"; and in some sports, such as baseball, it is an advantage to certain players, such as pitchers who, when they are cross-dominant, have their master eye closer to the plate.

A hunter who intends to use a bare bow or, for that matter, a shotgun, needs to determine which is his master eye and if it conforms with whatever kind of "handedness" he possesses. There's a very simple test for this, and it's one that should be conducted on any beginning shooter before he ever picks up a weapon.

To determine right- or left-eye dominance, cut a quarter-sized hole in a piece of paper or cardboard. Now have the person being tested hold the cardboard in both hands at waist level. With an observer 6 to 10 feet away and facing the test subject, the subject with both eyes open quickly brings the cardboard up to eye level at arms' length and looks through the hole. The observer can then note with which eye, right or left, the subject is viewing. This is the master eye. The test can also be performed without the use of a paper by having the subject overlap his two hands so that a hole is shaped by the webbing of those hands; holding the hands together, raise them again at arms' length and look at the observer through the hole. The observer will again be able to register the subject's favoring of one eye over the other, except in those rare and disturbing ambivisual instances in which the subject demonstrates no discernable preference for either eye.

If a hunter discovers cross-dominance early enough, he can consider switching over his bow or shotgun (it's less of a factor when using rifles or handguns with iron sights or scopes), so that he is shooting from the side of his master eye. If, on the other hand, a hunter has been shooting right-handed for some time and discovers he is actually left-eye dominant, then he does have options. Short of retraining himself to use his weapon from the other side of his body, he can, on a bow, go to pins and a peep sight (in fact, for the cross-dominant archer there's very little other choice). For the birdhunter, wearing

A simple test for determining the master eye.

shooting glasses and taping out the cross-dominant eye can force the other eye to take over sighting duties while preserving peripheral vision. Just a small circle of frosted tape on the lens over the iris of the master eye will let a hunter shoot with both eyes open and eliminate his mixed laterality. In time, a shooter may learn that by slightly squinting his dominant eye he can shift his visual focus over to the opposite side and still receive the benefit of binocular vision.

The basic visual skills needed by hunters are the same as those needed by anyone engaging in any sporting activity. The list of these skills would include "dynamic visual acuity," which is being able to see objects clearly when they are in motion; "eye tracking," which is being able to keep up with an object with your eyes when it is in motion; "eye focusing," which is quickly changing focus from one distance to another; "peripheral vision," which lets one be aware of his surroundings when he is looking straight ahead; "fusion," "flexibility," and "stamina," which translated means that the eyes are working together; "depth perception," which tells one how far away something is and how fast it is moving; and "visualization," which is the "being the target" thing that lets a hunter imagine the act of pointing/aiming a hunting weapon, firing it, and envisioning the successful result.

All of these skills depend on eyes that are healthy and well cared for. The first step in seeing to that is to receive regular eye exams from an ophthalmologist. He's the only one who can give you a true gauge of the condition of your eyes and eyesight and detect problems ranging from glaucoma to cataracts and infections. Beyond that, there are a number of steps in terms of diet and exercise that you can take to preserve and improve the health of your eyes; *but before taking up any kind of new regime, be sure to consult your ophthalmologist first.*

Most of the steps you can take to ensure good eye health are little different from those taken to ensure the health of any organ of the body. A major cause of vision loss in older people is macular degeneration, which is the degeneration of the small central area of the retina, known as the *macula*. Some of the symptoms of macular degeneration include a distorting of straight lines, blurring of the center of vision, and a change in color perception. One of the best things to do to avoid this condition, as with so many others, is—surprise—*don't smoke* or certainly quit right now. Heavy drinking also has the potential to mess up your vision, even after you sober up, although a daily glass of red wine, because it is an antioxidant, may improve eye health.

From a nutritional standpoint, a variety of foods is at least speculated to be of value to your eyes and vision. There is the legend, of course, of the carrot. A Vitamin A deficiency can lead to lower levels of light-sensitive molecules in the eyes and therefore reduced night vision; so carrots, rich in this nutrient, have long been considered a cure. In World War II, fighter pilots munched on carrots religiously for this reason. On the other hand, extremely high doses of Vitamin A, such as the concentrated levels found in dog and polar-bear livers and diagnosed rather after the fact by the unfortunate poisoning of Antarctic explorers early in the last century, can be deadly. There is enough Vitamin A already in the average diet to make supplementing it unnecessary unless you just can't live without carrots.

One carotenoid and antioxidant that is generally lacking in the American diet and that may promote healthy eyes is lutein. Lutein (pronounced *LOO-teen*) is found in the dark pigments of green, leafy vegetables and some fruits and nuts. Along with possibly reducing the risk of macular degeneration, lutein filters the high-energy blue light that is believed to bring about "oxidative stress." It has been suggested that, at a minimum, 6 to 10 milligrams of lutein should be consumed per day. Probably the best source for it is cooked greens such as collard, turnip, spinach, and especially kale, which cooked provides 11.9 milligrams per half-cup and 26.5 milligrams per cup when eaten raw—and who can say "no" to raw kale? Thankfully, other vegetables and fruits, including broccoli, corn, oranges, and papayas, provide some lutein, as do egg yolks. And besides your lutein, don't forget a weekly portion or two of oily fish; the omega-3 fatty acid in it seems to be the sovereign remedy for all that ails everyone these days, including macular degeneration.

Nutritional supplements to benefit the eyes should be considered after achieving a healthy diet, but they should not necessarily be overlooked, either. And what about exercise? Are there ways to give your eyes a good workout?

Certainly the eye can be described as being very nearly muscle-bound.

There are all those extraocular muscles that move the eye around in almost every possible direction in its socket, plus the muscles that operate the lens, and the iris, a muscle itself. All muscles can profit from exercise, but are there calisthenics for eyes?

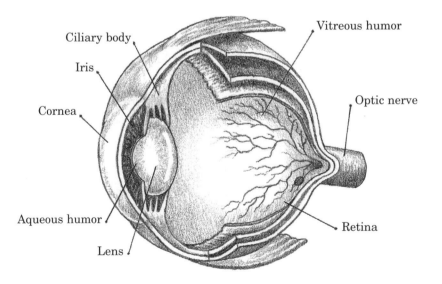

The hunter's first and truest optical device, the human eye.

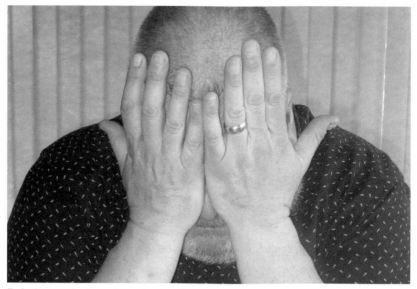

Palming technique for relaxing the eyes.

There is, in fact, a variety of exercises that can relieve the "eyestrain" produced by working indoors under artificial light. Moistening the eyes with their own tears, by blinking or yawning, helps. There is also a technique known as "palming," which involves resting your elbows on the edge of the desk and cupping your palms over your closed eyes as you lean forward, resting your head in your hands. You then inhale slowly through your nose, hold for a few seconds, then exhale, repeating for half a minute or so. And just getting out into the daylight can help remedy the ill effects of incandescent and fluorescent light.

In terms of actual exercises, one involves covering one eye and using the other to view objects at various focal distances in rapid succession, then switching to the other side. Or with both eyes closed, move them gently up and down and right to left behind the lids, repeating several times. Another training method is to hold the index finger near the eye and, while focusing on it, to move it slowly in and out, then focus on farther objects and back to the finger; then do this with the other eye.

Over the years there have been a number of courses of exercise outlined specifically to improve shooters' eyesight or, rather, their eye-hand coordination, it being impossible to have one without the other. It's hard to recommend any single regimen. It could be worthwhile to search the Internet, particularly in conjunction with the makers of shooting glasses, to find out if they have exercises they would suggest specifically for shooters. One such exercise used by a gold-medalist trap shooter involved placing a piece of paper with a large red dot on it on the wall. Then, *with an unloaded shotgun,* the shooter would step back; with both eyes open he would visually cover the red dot with the muzzle of his shotgun, holding the butt between his elbow and armpit, then raise the butt to his shoulder and the comb to his cheek, his eye forming the rear sight as it does in shotgun shooting, all the while the muzzle remaining unmoved in relation to the spot. He'd then lower the gun and repeat the exercise, often for hours at a time, until his hands and eyes automatically brought the gun to a proper mounted position.

Another interesting visual exercise comes from the world of racquetball. A champion player contends that because Westerners view most things from left to right, based on Western reading and writing style, they suffer from a weakened sense of seeing and tracking objects moving in the opposite direction. To better balance his skills between left to right and right to left, the racquetballer began writing in longhand in mirror image, à la Leonardo da Vinci. He then turned his books upside down, reading from left to right and bottom to top. He claims to have read three hundred volumes this way, often turning them upright every thirty minutes so he didn't overstrengthen either side.

There is a great deal that can be done to preserve our first and best optical devices through natural means. In the end, though, we will all, to a greater or lesser degrees, need to rely upon artificial ways of correcting, protecting, and improving our vision, particularly our hunting and shooting vision.

SIDELIGHT:

To judge the capabilities of the naked eye as an optical instrument, you need to consider only the thousands of years of extremely accurate astronomical observations that were made with it. The Maya, for instance, are believed to have identified the Orion nebula as something other than a single point of light centuries before the invention of the telescope, which made it possible to confirm the cloudlike structure of its stars.

Temple of the Giant Jaguar, Tikal, Guatemala; many Mayan buildings also served as observatories.

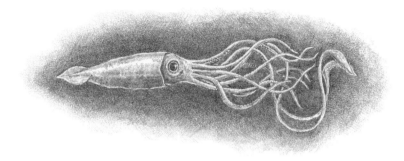

The largest eye in nature today belongs to the giant squid.

When it comes to the *largest* eyes in nature, though, humans lag well behind. The biggest eye ever to exist is said to have been that of a fishlike marine reptile known as *Temnodontosaurs platydon*, its 250-million-year-old fossil bones indicating a diameter of 26.4 centimeters. A close second is the estimated size of the eye of *Architeuthis*, the extant giant squid of Captain Nemo fame, thought possibly to reach 25 centimeters in the largest specimens.

PROTECTIVE EYEGLASSES

2

Yoked to the concept of vision is *optics*. Derived from the Greek word for vision, *optikos*, "optics" can be defined as the physical science that deals with the origins, properties, behavior, and phenomena of light. The science of optics separates into two distinct fields. One is "physical optics," which is about the nature of light—all those waves and particles and quanta—and one of the more quarrelsome and ancient questions of physics and so not the subject of this book. The other is "geometrical optics," which deals with the manner in which images are formed by lenses, mirrors, prisms, etc. It is this second field of optics that is of concern here, in particular as another definition of the word when applied to all the optical instruments and devices used to correct, enhance, and extend vision, especially the sporting optics used in hunting.

The study of geometrical optics goes back at least twenty-three hundred years to the Greek geometer Euclid, who discussed perspective and other observable qualities of light in terms of "visual rays." Later scientists, such as Ptolemy in the AD second century, continued the study of optics while still believing that visual rays are emitted from the eyes at extreme velocities and go to the objects being seen, rather than light traveling from the objects to the eyes. Even when thinking in terms of visual rays, Ptolemy still accurately examined both reflection and refraction—the slowing and bending of light as it passes through materials of different densities, such as from air to water: Think of a car driving fast down a straight road and running into a deep puddle of water; the car strikes the puddle and is slowed and thrown off its original course, resuming its original velocity when it leaves the water; something similar takes place with light when it passes from one medium to another.

Different media have different slowing effects on light, and the factor by which a material slows light is known as its "index of refraction"—expressed by some number greater than one. Ptolemy was measuring these indexes almost two millennia ago, and the values he calculated remain very close to modern ones.

In the eleventh century the Iraqi physicist Abu Ali al-Hassan Ibn al-Haitham, who would be known to Europeans as "Alhazen," put an end to the nonsense of visual rays streaming from the eye. In his great work, *Kitab-al-Manadhirn,* the *Book of Optics,* he made it clear that the eye is merely a passive receptor that is struck by and records the light reflected from objects or emanating from a source such as the sun or a candle. He also described the eye as an instrument comprised of a lens, iris, and so on. For more than half a millennium his work exerted significant influence over other scientists, among them the seventeenth-century German astronomer Johannes Kepler, whom some credit with having devised the modern scientific method of taking large amounts of imperfect data and refining them to arrive at a basic natural law.

One of the other refractive materials studied by Ptolemy was glass. It is the ability of glass, in the shape of a lens, to concentrate or diverge light rays that is, of course, the core of optics in the sense of sporting optics. Minus the glass lens, at least until the arrival of the plastic one, there was no discussion of such optics to be had.

Glass is a very old material, believed to have originated during the fourth millennium BC. There is no factual way of knowing precisely who invented it back in the Bronze Age, but there are fanciful-sounding theories about how Phoenician mariners discovered it when they cooked on the beach, and the sand beneath their fires melted. The first lenses, though, were probably not glass but rather gemstones or quartz. These were polished, originally, as jewelry or to decorate mummy cases as the twinkling eyes of the carved personage on the lid.

No doubt by accident, the optical qualities of polished, rounded, translucent stones were recognized; and there is evidence, excavated from the ruins of ancient Nineveh and dating back to 640 BC, of a crystal being shaped into a lens. Such lenses, and later glass ones, may have been used, as described by the Greek satirical playwright Aristophanes, as a "burning glass"—a magnifier to focus the light and ignite tinder. Yet, there is also the tale of the Emperor Nero's taking in a gladiatorial exhibition while peering, presumably myopically, through a lens of polished emerald.

The medieval illuminators of sacred texts are said to have used "reading stones," glass orbs sliced in half, to assist them in their work by enlarging the writings they were transcribing. Eyeglasses were the next logical progression; and there is no doubt a tavern, somewhere, in which a spirited wager or two may be placed on whom, exactly, invented them. The period around the end of the thirteenth century seems fairly reliable; and there is the legend of the Florentine Dominican friar who whipped up a pair for a physicist friend of his who had damaged his eyesight by conducting light experiments; but don't be surprised if someone else says it was the thirteenth-century genius English friar, "the Admirable Doctor," Roger Bacon, or some anonymous astronomer from far-off Cathay.

By theoretical definition, a normal eye is one in which the light from an infinitely distant object focuses clearly on the retina when the eye is in a relaxed state of accommodation (*see below for explanation of "accommodate"*). This is known as *emmetropia* ("well-proportioned eye"). Malformation of the eye, *ametropia* (an eye "without measure" or out of proportion), is characterized by several conditions.

The eye "accommodates" to varying focal lengths by stretching the lens through the tightening of the ciliary body, and then letting it spring back to normal by relaxing the muscles. Certain conditions can make this difficult, though. The most common is *presbyopia* which is experienced in older age when the lens begins to lose its elasticity, and reading glasses become a fact of life. That good Italian friar was said to have made the glasses to aid his friend's *hyperopia* ("long eye," or farsightedness), though it's difficult to envision how the physicist could have acquired this condition by accident. Farsightedness is caused by the focal length of the eye being naturally too long to allow the diverging rays of light from near objects to focus sharply on the retina; the focus point would be past the retina. It is possible to squeeze, or accommodate, the eye's lens down to shorten the focal length, but this generally results in eyestrain and headaches. Glasses with convex lenses, such as the friar's supposed invention—and today made in the proper prescription strength—converge the light rays at a reduced distance and allow the eye to remain relaxed.

Likewise, *myopia* (from the Greek word *muÿps,* meaning "nearsightedness" and also called "short eye"; myopia derives from a focal length too *short* to allow distant objects to reach the retina clearly) can be corrected with the use of concave lenses. Developed in the early fourteenth century and immortalized in Raphael's portrait of a bespectacled Pope Leo X and transformed into a demonic grotesquery by the notorious twentieth-century Irish-born British painter Francis Bacon, concave lenses extend the focal length so it falls sharply on the retina. It took until the mid-eighteenth century for Benjamin Franklin to assemble both types of lenses, convex and concave, in one set of frames and present the world with bifocal glasses.

A third condition, requiring corrective lenses that do not necessarily converge or diverge, is *astigmatism,* Greek for, essentially, "pointless." Astigmatism is brought about by a defect in, or distortion of, usually, the cornea, thus preventing light rays from focusing on one point of the retina and resulting in blurred vision. In the early nineteenth century the English astronomer Sir George Biddle Airy, afflicted with astigmatism himself, designed glasses to remedy the condition: The area of the cornea containing the irregularity is located, and a corresponding place in the eyeglass lens is ground to focus the light properly and overcome the distortion.

All of these vision problems, and others such as color blindness, are correctible both by glasses and contact lenses (originally conceived of by Leonardo da Vinci) and in some cases by surgery. Keen vision is a prerequisite for good hunting and shooting; but there is an added consideration for the hunter, and that is the protection of the eye, which can be adequately ensured only by the use of well-made protective glasses. So, *and this cannot be emphasized too strongly,* the first real item of sporting optics that needs to be considered is protective, or shooting, glasses because they are absolutely the first and most important man-made optical device that any hunter can have and use—*must* use.

As a hunter, even if you don't need corrective lenses, you do need protective ones—think *hunting with Dick Cheney*. Industrial safety glasses have to conform to rigorous testing guidelines established by the Occupational Safety and Health Administration (OSHA) or the American National Standards Institute (ANSI). Most eyeglass lenses today qualify under the Food and Drug Administration's (FDA) lesser standards for impact resistance. The steps of the FDA's lens-impact test are set down as follows:

a 5/8-inch steel ball weighing approximately 0.56 ounce is dropped from a height of 50 inches upon the horizontal upper surface of the lens. The ball shall strike within a 5/8-inch diameter circle located at the geometric center of the lens. The ball may be guided but not restricted in its fall by being dropped through a tube extending to within approximately 4 inches of the lens. To pass the test, the lens must not fracture; for the purpose of this section, a lens will be considered to have fractured if it cracks through its entire thickness, including a laminar layer, if any, and across a complete diameter into two or more separate pieces, or if any lens material visible to the naked eyes becomes detached from the ocular surface . . .

Anyway, that's the idea.

It's really not an overly reassuring degree of protection and in fact does not offer genuine protection against a load of birdshot. What are needed are not merely impact-resistant glasses but rather shooting glasses that have stamped on them the ANSI safety rating of "Z87.1" or "Z87.1 +" (indicating glasses made for high impact), meaning they have passed the institute's test for "occupational and educational" eye protection. Some shooting glasses may bear the claim that their *frames* pass the ANSI test. Tests have shown that Z87.1 *lenses* should protect a shooter's eyes against No. 8 shot fired from as close as 15 yards.[i] What Z87.1 *frames* protect is anybody's guess. *Caveat emptor,* to say the least.

There are several choices of lens material for hunting-shooting glasses. No one really seems to be making them out of glass anymore, so that's not likely a decision that will need to be made. Today most lenses, especially in sporting eyewear, are made of plastic of one type or another:

- There is **Plastic CR-39** (*CR* being the abbreviation of "Columbia Resin"), which is "economical" and offers the least impact resistance.
- The strongest material for lenses is **polycarbonate,** an extremely impact-resistant thermoplastic that is thinner and lighter than Plastic CR-39.
- An even thinner and lighter impact-resistant material is **polycarbonate 1.0,** well-suited for shooters who need stronger prescriptions in a manageable weight.
- Then there is **high-index plastic,** not as impact resistant as polycarbonate 1.0 but similar in thickness and weight and believed to offer the best optics among plastic lenses.

Look for a "Z87" certification on shooting glasses.

A universal failing of plastic lenses is a tendency to scratch rather easily. When buying any glasses that you will be subjecting to rough conditions, be sure that they have a scratch-resistant coating.

The curvature of the lenses is another important consideration. Eyeglasses advance from "plano" lenses—flat planes— through head-hugging wraparounds that are known as an "eight-base" curve. Most traditional-style hunting-shooting glasses are essentially plano, harking back to when impact-resistant lenses had to be made from *crown glass,* an exceptionally hard and clear soda-lime optical glass with a relatively low refractive index *(see discussion of Ptolemy and "index of refraction" earlier in this chapter)* and low dispersion *(see discussion of low-dispersion glass in Chapter 3).* And this is the style that many traditionalist hunters prefer. Their arguments for flatter glasses have to do with feelings of inadequacy—no, no, it's about some shooters' feeling that they are "closed in" by wraparound glasses, that they will sacrifice their peripheral vision. Plano

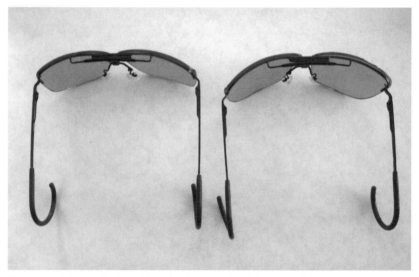

The metal-framed shooting glasses on the left are a 6-base curve, while those on the right are a more aggressive 8-base curve.

lenses in metal frames are not qualified to be rated by ANSI, and they don't seem to do that well in impact tests; many foreign objects, whether stray shot from the side, hot gases, metal shavings, or even twigs and sticks when walking, in short, anything that might assault a hunter's eyes, are not necessarily going to hit only face-on. (Of late, curved lenses up to eight-base are being fitted into time-honored metal frames.)

Wraparounds today can be completely clear and distortion-free where they bend around the face, without limiting peripheral vision in any way. And by wrapping around, they can provide full protection for a hunter's complete eye, not merely his cornea. Puncturing the sclera, the "white" of the eye, and the other two *tunics* that maintain the eyeball's integrity and losing the vitreous humor are just as blinding as injuring the lens. Not fully protecting the eye can be like buying half a sleeping bag for Arctic survival.

Shooting glasses may be completely clear. Or there is a vast array of shades in which they can be tinted. Any tinting, though, will reduce the amount of visible light reaching the eye, which will in turn cause the iris to expand. A more-open iris allows added amounts of ultraviolet light rays, such as UVA and UVB, to enter the eye. These invisible rays are what cause sunburns and other types of skin damage and so are not beneficial to have flooding into the eye. Glass does not filter out UVA, but plastics do filter out at least some UVA and UVB and in some cases all ultraviolet rays. Price, by the way, is really no guarantee that a pair of shooting glasses will filter UV effectively. Cheap drugstore sunglasses may filter out as much as do a pair of $400 fashion-statement Italian imports. When purchasing shooting glasses, make sure the label states that they filter out 100 percent of UV.

As for tints, hunters and shooters can choose from dozens. Simple sunglasses should not be equated with protective shooting glasses. The dark-gray or dark-green tints of sunglasses make them suitable for driving on sunny days, but they are probably not the best choice for picking up a flushing quail or a glint of antler across a draw, although they will camouflage a hunter's eyes if he's trying to draw in game to close range, such as a deer coming to antler rattling or a turkey to a call. (Also there are certain tints that shooting glasses may come in, such as some blues, that are excellent for spotting clay targets but are not recommended for wearing behind the wheel of an automobile.)

Unfortunately, there really isn't a one-tint-fits-all for hunting-and-shooting glasses. From clear, tints can run from pale yellow to vermillion (good for hunters with red-green color blindness) to dark purple, with one tint working better than another, depending on light conditions. So for shooting orange skeet targets on a cloudy gray day, hunter orange might be the tint of choice. Duck hunting over water on a bluebird day might call for a polarized brown or bronze—waterfowlers, though, should be careful not to flare the birds by looking up too soon and having the sun glare off their glasses, though it is possible to buy lenses with antireflective coatings. And a big-game hunter might go with a light amber-rose to pick up the contrasts of animals against a background of trees or brush.

A hunter and recreational shooter should probably have three pairs of glasses or glasses with interchangeable lenses in three different tints to cover most types and times of day and shooting activities. For all types of shooting, clear or light yellow would be sensible for early mornings and late evenings, under overcast skies, or in bad weather. These would also work at an indoor shooting range or for safety when handloading. For outdoor target shooting, at the rifle or pistol range, or the trap-and-skeet or sporting-clays course, a shade of orange ought to be in order. And for going afield after game, a hunter should have two shades of glasses: the clear or pale yellow for dusk and dawn and something along the lines of the light amber-rose, mentioned earlier, for the bright light of midday.

Frame type is another issue. As previously noted, plano glasses will likely have metal frames, but metal frames may also hold the various curved lenses. In most cases, and while they are more fragile than other kinds, metal frames are usually the most adjustable, letting a hunter fine-tune the temples and, in glasses with adjustable nose pads, the height of the glasses[ii] until arriving at the perfect fit for himself. There could be a problem, though: Many people have an allergy to the nickel found in most metal frames. A hunter can apply clear nail polish to the parts of the frames—*not* the lenses—that touch his skin as an antinickel coating, though it can later be hard to remove from the frames and may not look overly stylish. Another option is titanium frames, which are strong, light, fully adjustable, and nonallergenic, as well as expensive. Nylon frames, such as those found on most wraparounds, will be the most durable and generally do allow a certain amount of adjustment. Being flexible, extremely

Wraparound shooting glasses can provide fuller protective covering.

light, and fitting tightly to the head, they are not likely to fly off when the game's afoot.

As far as earpieces ("temples") go, options begin with "skull" temples, the rigid, bent kind found on most eyeglasses. These are usually very comfortable and hold the glasses on well. "Bayonet" temples are straight and made for easy on and off, such as for reading glasses. Wraparounds with nylon frames tend to have bayonet temples, but, again, these types of glasses depend mostly on their spring tension to keep themselves in place. The last choice is probably the most secure but potentially the least comfortable, and that is the "cable" temple. This is the kind of hook-around-the-ear wire frame often seen on aviator glasses. They will indeed hold a hunter's glasses in place, but if the hooks are not flexible enough or without a soft-plastic coating, or if the temples are too short and so pull against the ears, they can become quite annoying, and even painful, to wear. For those who wear a belt and suspenders, a retaining strap can be attached to the temples to hold the glasses on. Retainers come in a variety of kinds, including neoprene rubber, and ones that will keep your glasses afloat if they somehow fly off your face and into the duck pond.

If a hunter does not need vision correction, or if he does and already wears contact lenses, then optically clear glasses are fine, and these could be the kind of plastic ones sold in bulk in cellophane wrappers in gunshops. If a hunter with a vision problem wears glasses instead of contacts, there are also oversized tinted safety covers that can be placed over glasses, but this is a pretty much jury-rigged solution. The most straightforward answer is prescription shooting glasses. Many manufacturers of top-quality shooting glasses offer prescriptions as an added feature. Plano glasses can have the prescriptions ground right into the tinted lens. For most wraparounds that offer prescriptions, though, a sort of pince-nez insert that snaps onto the nose piece is available. These tend to be somewhat distracting because the edges of the insert lenses can be in the field of vision. Currently at least one manufacturer of wraparound shooting glasses, Hidefspex, can have a prescription added to its lenses, without an insert, and more manufacturers are following suit.

If a hunter normally wears bifocals or glasses with progressive lenses, the idea of having shooting glasses made this way may seem sensible. Au contraire, bifocals in the field are too clever by half. Every time a gun is raised, a hunter will invariably be looking through the close-focusing portion of the lens, which he'll also be looking through when he's walking, making the broken ground beneath his feet appear to be pitching away like a funhouse floor. It is better to stick with lenses that are made in a single, distance prescription. If a hunter needs near vision on occasion in the field, there are magnifying lenses, such as those used by fly fishermen, which can be attached to the eyeglass frame or to the brim of a cap and flipped down when the situation calls for them.

One more consideration for hunters when it comes to glasses is fogging. If hunters exert themselves in the field, they are at the very least going to steam up. Even when a hunter is sitting in stand on a cold day, there can be a significant variance between the air temperature and the temperature of his skin; and this can cause glasses to cloud over. This is probably the single greatest reason why so many pairs of shooting glasses remain in their cases when hunters enter the woods. Some glasses do come with antifogging and water-shedding coatings applied by the manufacturers. The best solution for avoiding fogging, though, is a design that allows the glasses to sit on the face both securely but with enough of an opening around the lenses to let air circulate freely. Plano glasses are the best for this, and many wraparounds also allow proper circulation. Some, which seal to the face with rubber gaskets, have vents to maintain airflow. A hunter, though, should try on any pair of shooting glasses he is considering purchasing to see if the lenses will receive adequate ventilation.

Keeping hunting-shooting glasses clean is vital and can help prevent fogging. In cleaning plastic lenses, including poly-carbonate, care must be taken not to polish grit right into them. Before cleaning, lenses need to have any dust removed from them, which can be accomplished with a lens brush, often called a "lens pen." The most thorough and safest way to avoid lens scratches from cleaning is to wash shooting glasses under running water with a mild liquid soap. The lenses can be flushed under the tap to wash away any particles of dust, then a drop of soap can be applied to all the surfaces. A hunter can use his clean fingers to wash the lenses gently under the water, not forgetting the frames, nose pads, and temples, too, and then rinse them. For drying, a soft, clean, grit-free and lint-free cloth may be used. This could be a lens-cleaning cloth from the optician's office or one sold in a camera store. An old cotton T-shirt, though, one

A basic lens-cleaning kit should consist of, from left to right, a soft, lint-free cloth, cleaning fluid, and a lens pen.

that's gone through the Whirlpool many times, can also be soft enough to dry and polish lenses. Just don't overdo the buffing.

Lens-cleaning towelettes in individual packets are available, and spray-on and rub-on antifogging concoctions are also on the market; but again, glasses have to be dust-free before these are applied. As was said in the introduction, this book is not about the naming of specific brands and models, at least not in a comprehensive, and therefore, inevitably transitory buyer's-guide sense. Change happens. So while Major Sir Gerald Burrard's *Notes on Sporting Rifles* remains of genuine value to the rifle-hunter of today, over half a century since it was published, the 1998 edition of the *Shooter's Bible* is of interest chiefly as a curiosity. All of which leads to the exception that proves the rule, about not naming products, the earlier mention of particular shooting glasses and, not counting a household appliance.

Over twenty years ago Ed Kalbach, working in a ski shop in Logan, Utah, noticed that sunglasses accounted for a large number of purchases. He began to devise various accessories for

Cat Crap.

sunglasses, one of them a kind of balm made from a mild soap ingredient. This substance could be applied to clean lenses and then wiped off with a soft cloth, leaving the lenses clear and fog resistant. This antifog product was packaged in quarter-ounce containers and became the basis for Kalbach's company, EK Ekcessories, Incorporated. The product, which works quite well, is Cat Crap, explaining why it was impossible not to include its name in these pages.

SIDELIGHT:

A famous eye injury that could have been prevented through the wearing of safety glasses was the one suffered by the naturalist and founder of the Sierra Club (and a man perhaps not so well known for having said, "Interest in hunting is almost universal, so deeply is it rooted as an inherited instinct ever ready to rise and make itself known"), John Muir. As a young man working in a mill in Indiana he pierced his right eye with a file "just where the cornea meets the sclerotic coating," blinding that eye. With time and the invaluable aid of his friend Catharine Merrill, who took him to the best oculist in Indianapolis for treatment, Muir regained the sight in his eye. The accident, though, inspired him to embark on his forty-year odyssey through the wilderness of North America, resulting in such unmatched works of nature writing as *The Mountains of California, Our National Parks, My First Summer in the Sierra, Steep Trails, Stickeen,* and others.

THE SPOTTING SCOPE

3

alileo Galilei (born 1564 in Pisa, Italy, and often called the "father of science") is widely believed to have had the telescope spring fully armed from his head, to the unsurpassed outrage of the Roman Catholic Church. The truth is that Galileo had a considerable amount of optical help extending far back into history. And it may be that his "invention" was not so outrageous to the Church, after all.

The Galilean telescope is, though, the basis for all of the sporting optics used by hunters in the field. Without the *telescope* (from the Greek for "farseeing") there would be no spotting scope, no binocular (more about that spelling later), or riflescope. What is it that the telescope does? It magnifies distant objects. What, then, is *magnification?*

The root of the word lies, of course, in the Latin *magnus,* meaning "great" or "large." From *magnus* comes a Middle English word meaning "to extol" or "lift up." In terms of optics, as the word is used in this book, magnification is determined by the *focal length* (the distance from the optical center of the lens to the principal point of focus, i.e., how many millimeters from the flat plane slicing vertically through the middle of the lens to the point in the air where the converging rays meet in sharp focus) of the eyepiece, combined with the focal length (from the optical center of the front lens to the principal point of focus of the light rays converging inside the instrument) of the instrument to which the eyepiece is attached. Okay, simplified, magnification means the ability of an optical instrument to make an object appear closer than it appears to the unaided eye. In telescopes and binoculars, etc., this is expressed as a *power,* designated by a numeral and the symbol *X,* such as "8X" or "10X," and thought by many to represent a factor of enlargement in which the image is made eight or ten times bigger. Would that it were so.

If an image is made larger, such as the picture of a 6-foot-tall man projected onto a movie screen so that he becomes 20 feet tall, that is called *linear magnification.* The magnification produced by a telescope, though, is not about real images but rather virtual ones. With a telescope, images seen through the eyepiece can actually be no bigger than a few millimeters, yet the way they appear to the eye is the result of *angular magnification.* To understand angular magnification, it is first necessary to understand *subtension,* an important concept also (as will be shown) for getting the most out of a riflescope.

While some animals (for the most part birds) enjoy a field of vision approaching 360 degrees, the binocular vision of humans covers an arc of about 140 degrees. Most of that 140 degrees is taken up by peripheral vision, and only some 6 degrees, or just over 4 percent of the total visual field, will be in sharp focus. In physical terms, this means that on a page of normal-sized print held at arm's length roughly five words would be readable at one time without shifting the gaze. So it could be said that those five words "subtend" 6 degrees of arc. Or think of the night sky directly overhead as a horizon-to-horizon arc of 180 degrees. A full moon in that sky, at about a quarter-million miles from the Earth, covers 0.54 degrees, or just 0.3 percent, of that arc (and the sun, at an average distance of 92 million miles, covers almost exactly the same amount, making total solar eclipses possible). At arm's length, an upraised thumb will just cover the moon in the sky; the moon, by the way, remains the same size throughout its passage—even if it appears larger as it rises, it does not exceed that same thumb's width.

In angular magnification, then, it is not the size of the object but rather the angle that it *subtends* that is enlarged, and as a result the area of the retina that is covered as well. Seen through a 10X telescope (and needless to say, don't try this with the sun), the moon's 0.54 degree of arc will be widened ten times to 5.4 degrees, near to that 6 degrees arc of optimum focus in the human field of vision. It would be like moving the word "Copernicus" toward oneself until, assuming one's eyes could accommodate properly, it looked like

Copernicus.

Figuratively speaking, an image in a telescope is not made larger; it is brought closer—through the widening of the arc it subtends and the greater area of the retina it covers.

As has been noted, the magnifying lens is of ancient origin, yet so, too, may be the telescope. Some speculate that a rock-crystal lens found in Assyrian ruins dating back more than three thousand years could have been a component of a telescope. This speculation is evidenced by the Assyrians' supposed advanced knowledge of astronomy, such as the existence of the rings that encircle Saturn, which they described as "serpents." Another possible example of the antiquity of the telescope is other rock-crystal (quartz) artifacts, known as the "Visby lenses," discovered in a tenth-century Viking grave on the Swedish island of Gotland in the Baltic Sea. Some of these very sophisticated lenses were mounted in silver, leading to the conjecture that they might have been from a telescope. The raw quartz they are made from is not present in Gotland but rather appears to be from the Black Sea region; and so the lenses might have been crafted by Persians or Arabs, who were far more advanced and adept at astronomy than the face-painting, hut-dwelling Europeans of the era.

The telescope definitely emerges, though, around the end of the sixteenth and the beginning of the seventeenth centuries. The English mathematician and surveyor (and unsuccessful rebel against Queen Mary) Leonard Digges is credited by some with having invented the telescope in the 1570s, as well as the theodolite (a word of his own coinage) for measuring vertical and horizontal angles to specific landmarks to aid him in his survey work.

After Digges, the discoverers *in dubio* were a trio of Dutch spectacle masters. Two children playing in Hans Lippershey's Middelburg shop are said to have seen that images were larger and clearer when viewed through two lenses rather than one. This observation, so the story goes, led Lippershey (or Lipperhey, according to other spellings) to construct a "device by means of which all things at a very large distance can be seen as if they were nearby." Lippershey placed this device, which he called a *kijkglas,* or "look glass," and which had a magnification of around 3X, in his shop, pointed to the church tower across town and used it as a roadside attraction to lure in customers. Lippershey applied for a thirty-year patent for his *kijkglas* in 1608, drawing the notice of two other opticians, Jacob Metius and Zacharias Janssen, who had apparently been working on telescopes of their own, all three independently of one another. Consequently, no one "inventor" was awarded a patent. (It also didn't help anybody's petition that toy telescopes, it seems, were already being sold on the streets of Paris.)

In Venice in 1609 Galileo heard word of these new Dutch instruments and came up with a better design of his own, using a convex lens for the *aperture* or *objective,* the big end of the instrument that is pointed at, and nearest to, the object being viewed, and a concave lens for the *ocular,* the eyepiece. He called his innovation a *perspicullum* and later by the Italian word *telescopio,* which became "telescope" in English. He presented an 8X model of his telescope to the Venetian senate and went on to build telescopes up to 20X with which he made his famous celestial observations.

Within two years Johannes Kepler had improved on Galileo by building a telescope made with two convex lenses, front and back, providing increased magnification, a much larger field of view, and longer eye relief (the latter two subjects to be examined in further detail in following chapters). The one drawback of the Keplerian telescope was that the image emerging from the eyepiece was inverted instead of upright. Kepler later demonstrated that the addition of a third convex lens, an *erector,* could reinvert the image; but the astronomers of the time preferred his two-lens

Galileo built his first telescopes out of wood and leather, to hold the lenses.

model due to the poor quality of seventeenth-century glass, choosing the man in the moon standing on his head over yet another badly distorting lens.

Both Kepler's and Galileo's telescopes were refracting or *dioptric* (Greek, again, "viewing through"). Galileo's could be used as a terrestrial, as well as an astronomical, telescope because of its erect image. The glass lenses of each, though, suffered from serious *chromatic aberration* (the breaking up of white light into its spectrum of hues, known as "dispersion"), seen as fuzzy "color fringing" in the images being viewed, the individual, and varied, color wavelengths unable to be brought into focus together. Around 1670 Sir Isaac Newton solved this problem by building the first useful reflecting or *catoptric* (from "mirror" in Greek) telescope, which did away with an objective lens and used a primary parabolic mirror to collect and focus the light on a smaller secondary flat diagonal mirror, which reflected it to an eyepiece. Thus, no more fringing.

A serious shortcoming of catoptric telescopes in the hunting field, or anywhere they need to be toted around, though, is their basic lack of durability. Mirrors don't travel well, being prone to breakage and all that attendant bad luck; and with a primary and secondary one, there is a constant problem of keeping the two aligned, or *collimated*. So for more than a century after Newton, the optics of choice for field observation remained the Galilean telescope, as exemplified by the swashbuckling pirate's spyglass, even though the first telescopes built by Lippershey under contract from the Netherlands' States General were binocular.

Chromatic aberration remained a serious problem until optics makers learned how to assemble an *achromatic* ("without color") *lens,* using a convex lens of crown glass and a concave one of flint glass (traditionally a high-dispersion and high-refractive potash-lead glass, now made with nontoxic metals substituting for the lead), fitted and cemented together in what is known as an *achromatic doublet*. Achromatic lenses work by bringing two different color wavelengths into shared focus.

The individual lenses, by the way, that make up *a single* "lens," such as the objective or the eyepiece, are known as *elements*. Elements assembled together, one behind the other, in a telescope or another optical device but not cemented together can be described as *groups*, as can two or more elements that *are* cemented together. So, the three separate elements and two joined elements, for example, making up an objective lens would be defined as *air spaced*, and the lens might be described as "an objective lens constructed of four air-spaced groups of five elements."

The total number of elements in an optical device is noteworthy, to a degree. In theory, the more elements in an optical device, the greater the reduction of aberration, both chromatic and *spherical aberration*, another focusing imperfection observed primarily at shorter distances and caused by the spherical shape of most lenses. This assumes the highest quality of optical glass being used for the elements, and even then each additional element can contribute a touch more reflection—and therefore greater flaring of the image and loss of light transmission. An optics maker might also employ the exceptionally large number of elements in his devices as an advertising pitch and fail to mention that they are all about the same quality as *kijkglas* lenses.

Beyond achromatic come *apochromatic lenses*, originally developed for microscopes, which can produce the focusing of three (red, green, and blue) or more wavelengths of light on the same point and so create an even sharper image. Apochromatic lenses, often designated as "APO," may use elements made from the artificial crystal fluorite and are found on high-quality optics (although there is some question about how loosely manufacturers may toss around the term and whether it is an absolute guarantee of quality or merely more optical smoke and, as it were, mirrors). There are other types of low-dispersion glass that are used in telescopes, etc., that may be labeled as *ED* ("extra-low dispersion") or *SLD* ("special low dispersion") or *HD* ("high definition") or something similar. Hunters, as much or more than any other users of optics, ideally want devices with the least possible amount of chromatic aberration; and low-dispersion glass is one of the features they should look for when purchasing a spotting scope.

Reflection is another concern. Reflection off the surface of a lens means less light reaching the viewer's eye. No real solution for this existed until the middle of the nineteenth century, when, it is believed, lens makers began to notice that glass that had taken on a discoloration, or "stain," from the grinding process somehow transmitted more light than did clear, unstained glass. Officially, it was John William Strutt, third baron of Rayleigh and thus an English nobleman and ultimately a Nobel man in physics, who in 1886 discovered that such a tarnish had an index of refraction falling somewhere between that of the air and the glass and so reduced reflection and let more light pass through.

Antireflective coatings, such as magnesium fluoride, can be applied to a lens surface in a layer as thin as two to three hundred-thousandths of a meter, increasing that lens' antireflectivity. The application of several layers is known as "multicoating" and can permit the transmission of more than 99 percent of direct visible light through *each lens surface*—each surface, though, will still reflect its own little portion of light, and rays coming in from oblique angles will bounce off more than direct ones, and glass itself actually absorbs some light; so considerably less than 99 percent of the light entering an optical device will come out through the eyepiece. Nanotechnology has recently made it possible to go beyond this through the use of porous silica and titanium-oxide nanorod layers, measuring 100 nanometers (one ten-millionth of a meter) in thickness, deposited on an aluminum-nitride film. This type of antireflective multicoating can absorb, and therefore transmit, 99.9 percent of all visible light from all angles and shows the potential of being 100 percent antireflective. Hunters should not rush over to Cabela's quite yet, though, because it will likely be some time before this type of coating appears on the lenses of spotting scopes or any other hunting optics.

Manufacturers presently use four designations for the coatings on their optics' lenses. These are:

- **Coated:** A single layer of coating has been lavishly slapped on at least one lens surface, somewhere.
- **Fully Coated:** A single layer has been applied to all the "air-to-glass" surfaces, which includes the two sides of any air-spaced elements inside the optics ("air" being a term of art because most good optics will be purged of atmospheric air and filled with an inert gas such as nitrogen to prevent internal fogging).
- **Multicoated:** Several layers of antireflective coating have been applied to at least one lens surface.
- **Fully Multicoated:** All air-to-glass surfaces have received multiple layers of antireflective coating.

Obviously, when considering which brand and model of optics, whether binocular, riflescope, or spotting scope, to purchase, one should make full multicoating an important factor in the final decision.

In the hierarchy of optics for hunters, with protective lenses being set aside, the spotting scope would rank third, behind the riflescope and the binocular, in terms of how essential it is to have in the field. The spotting scope is, by its nature, the most deliberate optical instrument a hunter will use. Yet, there are times and places where it can be the most indispensable, too.

A definition: A *spotting scope* is a *monocular* (single eyepiece) telescope used in hunting to view objects at distances at

The spotting scope, and a place where a hunter cannot do without one.

which they cannot be easily or clearly viewed with a binocular. Binoculars of up to 25X can be found, and there is a comfort, depth-of-field, and depth-perception advantage to being able to view with both eyes. Such binoculars are, though, generally heavier and bulkier than even the largest spotting scopes, too big to be held steadily by hand and just not powerful enough for the tasks to which a spotting scope may be assigned.

The construction of a spotting scope involves an eyepiece attached to a *housing,* or "body" or "barrel," which contains the elements of the objective lens and the focusing lens—which may also serve as an erector for the image. Otherwise, a *reflective prism* (a glass body through which light is reflected and redirected and which may or may not contain mirror-coated surfaces; more in the next chapter) will be used to right the image and send it to the eyepiece.

The magnifying power of the scope is determined by the eyepiece. Eyepieces can run from 20X to 60X or more and may be straight power or *variable* (often designated as "zoom"). In deciding on how much magnification is enough, one of the things that needs to be taken into account is the size of the objective. And at least a portion of the reason for that has to do with the physical characteristics of the iris and the pupil of the human eye.

The iris regulates the amount of light entering the eye by expanding or contracting the diameter of the pupil. For most people with normal eyes the range of this expansion and contraction is from 3 millimeters in the brightest light to 7 millimeters in the darkest, though as humans grow older their pupils tend to open less, so that a 5-millimeter diameter may become the maximum. Likewise, there is an actual physical diameter to the light that emerges from the eyepiece of a spotting scope or of any other optical device of the kind being discussed in this book.

Ideally, the diameter of the light emitted from a spotting scope's eyepiece (known as the *exit pupil*) would be large enough to match the diameter of the eye's pupil when fully expanded, as it would be in the dim light of dawn or dusk. Perhaps to understand this better it would be good to assume, for the moment, that Ptolemy was correct and that sight is a matter of visual rays traveling from the eye to an object. If those rays left the eye through a 7-millimeter pupil and then had to pass through a 3-millimeter hole, over 80 percent of those rays would be blocked. Now to refute Ptolemy, think of how sight actually works. If light is emitted in a 3-millimeter beam from an eyepiece and enters a 7-millimeter pupil, only some 18 percent of the pupil's light capacity is being utilized; or put another way, 82 percent is wasted. In fact, it's unlikely that any spotting scope will provide a full 7 millimeters of exit pupil or anything even near it, but some scopes will assuredly provide you with more than others.

To calculate the exit pupil of a spotting scope or any other optical device, the diameter of the objective, in millimeters, is divided by the power of magnification. For a spotting scope with an

80-millimeter objective and a 60X eyepiece, for example, the equation would look like:

Exit Pupil = 80 millimeters ÷ 60 = 1.33 millimeters

This is generally considered to be the bare minimum useful exit pupil for a spotting scope.

There is, naturally, an exception to calculating exit pupil. Low-power scopes—usually riflescopes—will deliver an exit pupil less than that at which the calculations would arrive. For example, a 1X dangerous-game riflescope may have a 24 millimeter objective. By the formula above, this should provide a whopping exit pupil of 24 millimeters. Swarovski Optik actually offers a scope in this configuration, but the company's technical data for it lists a "measly" exit pupil of 9.6 millimeters.

One of Swarovski's executives explained it this way: "A 24 millimeter exit pupil is not desirable or possible optically. Basically just pushing a wider beam of light through a scope is not the answer to getting a brighter image. At the lowest magnifications (1–2X) we have a light stop controlling the flow of light through the scope to give us the optimum optical performance. This is in direct relation to what is called effective objective diameter. An example of this can be seen with some of our scopes at their lowest magnification. The exit pupil is way off the standard calculation when we use the known objective diameter. The light stop has effectively controlled our objective diameter. This reduction is only necessary at the lowest magnifications, as we increase the magnification we increase the amount of effective objective diameter that we are using. The higher magnifications are where the larger objectives are needed to provide us with sufficient exit pupil."

Assuming sufficient exit pupil, how much power is "enough"? For a variable-power eyepiece a top magnification of

60X is about the maximum a hunter would want to consider. Extremely high magnifications will aggravate the unsteadiness of the image or the blurring effect of heat shimmer and present a narrower *depth of field* (with an object in focus, the depth of field is the distance in front of and behind it that is also in focus)—game can appear anywhere, and more often than not out of nowhere, so the greater the depth of field, the greater the chance of catching sight of something in an unsuspected location.

A general, well-founded, assumption is that high power, even with a large objective, means a smaller exit pupil, and so there is a reduced ability to use a spotting scope in those lowlight hours when game is most active. If exit pupil were the sole consideration, this would be completely true. Another factor describing the relationship between the objective and magnifying power, which can be looked at when evaluating a spotting scope or the other types of hunting optics, is the *twilight factor*.

Though it sounds as if it might be something from the Smith Corona of Rod Serling, twilight factor is actually another way of comparing the relative usefulness of different configurations of spotting scopes in low light. Like exit pupil, twilight factor can be calculated mathematically. The twilight factor of a spotting scope is found by multiplying the diameter, in millimeters again, of the objective by the power of magnification and determining the square root of this number. Worked out for the 60x80-millimeter scope used as an example earlier, the equation would be:

Twilight Factor = $\sqrt{80} \times 60 = \sqrt{4800} = 69.3$

Now compare that with a 40x60-millimeter scope with an exit pupil over 25 percent larger in area (though still only 1.5 millimeters in diameter). Its twilight factor would be:

$\sqrt{60} \times 40 = \sqrt{2400} = 48.9$

Twilight factor was a much more significant consideration before the advent of low-dispersion glasses and multicoatings, but it remains useful for comparison purposes—think of it as the raw horsepower of an engine. With a variable-power eyepiece of say 20–60X on a scope with an 80-millimeter objective, the exit pupil and the twilight factor at the lowest power would be 4 millimeters and 40, respectively. Now making the assumption—and it is a major one—that glass and coatings are of exactly equal quality, then it is worthwhile noting that a 60-millimeter scope with a 15–45X eyepiece, a typical configuration, with the power setting turned all the way down, will have an exit pupil of 4 millimeters (the same as the 80-millimeter scope described earlier), but the twilight factor will be only 30. It's a V-8 versus a straight-6, yet each has its individual usefulness.[iii]

The logical inference would be that the spotting scope with the largest objective (and so the least spherical aberration because aberration increases farther from the center of the lens, so the bigger lens, the greater the lens area without aberration) and the most powerful eyepiece, within the practical limits of what a hunter can carry and use, would always be the answer. This certainly seems so for professional hunting guides, whose incomes are based on their ability to recognize the most far-off specks as wild game. It is clearly financially worthwhile for them to hike the mountains with ten to fifteen pounds of the best spotting scope and tripod that money can buy in their backpacks. But is this an extreme to which the average hunter should also go?

The weight and bulk of a spotting scope should be balanced against what it may save in terms of steps and miles. Once on a woodland-caribou hunt in Newfoundland, a hunter was dismayed, and considerably disappointed, to learn that his guide had no spotting scope. The hunter had asked before coming up if he ought to bring one of his own but had been assured by the outfitter that the guide would have a scope. Instead, the total extent of the guide's hunting optics amounted to a cheap 7X binocular with appallingly scoured plastic lenses. The hunt turned into sighting the barely distinguishable white capes of the "stag" caribou in binoculars and then humping several miles across the tundra to get a decent look at the antlers, which invariably turned out to be of lesser quality. After several days—and far too many of these long-range reconnaissance patrols—the hunter settled for *a* caribou. *Any* spotting scope, not necessarily the biggest on Earth, would have been a more than acceptable burden under these circumstances, if it would have made it possible to locate a true trophy stag *without* having to walk down half-a-dozen nontrophies. Here a good lighter-weight 15–45x60-millimeter scope, for example, would have been a godsend.

The need for a spotting scope on wide-open tundra, on plains and prairies, and in mountains and deserts is evident; yet even for hunters in the eastern half of the country, with its dense broadleaf and piney woods, definite uses can still be found for one. There is, for instance, often a lot of scouting of very large farm fields, made easier and more effective with the use of a spotting scope. For spotting big, predominantly crepuscular whitetail bucks, a 10x50-millimeter binocular (about as large as most hunters would care to carry) will provide a generous 5-millimeter exit pupil, against the minimum 1.33 millimeter of a 60-millimeter scope set at 45X. But now look at the twilight factor of that scope—52—set against that of the binocular—22.4. Which device, the binocular or the spotting scope, will conceivably be better able to resolve whether it's an eight point or a ten point at 500 yards at 4:45 p.m. in northern Wisconsin in late November?[iv]

The truth is that it is not a matter of either/or. Every hunter, at some time, will have use for both. There are certain situations—still-hunting, in general, in which there may not be time to stop and set one up—in which a spotting scope is more of an option than a necessity, while a binocular is indispensable in almost all big-game hunting circumstances and even in more bird-hunting circumstances than might be suspected—finding potholes where the ducks are "pitching in," as the saying goes Down South, and spotting turkeys strutting or on the roost come to mind. However often or seldom a spotting scope is used in the field by a hunter, it must be as rugged as any of the other optical devices being carried.

A reliable spotting scope should be guaranteed waterproof and fogproof. On top of that, many spotting scopes are *rubber armored* (the housings coated in a protective layer of synthetic rubber), which can absorb some shocks and dings if the scope gets bounced around. Because no armoring can prevent serious damage if the abuse is severe enough, some level of reasonably careful handling is required by all optics. For hiking, a scope ought to have additional protection beyond being dropped into a backpack with a tripod, skinning knives, and a Spam sandwich wrapped in wax paper. Most scopes will come from the manufacturer with padded nylon-cloth pouches to cover them, and there are neoprene "stay-on" covers (a sort of Body Glove™ for a scope) that can be folded away from the objective and ocular and remain on while the scope is in use.

During World War II the Martin B-26 bomber was dubbed the "Flying Prostitute" because the aircraft's critically small wing area made it look as if it had "no visible means of support." In using a spotting scope, especially at higher powers, it's critical to have very visible and very solid support for it. A camera tripod is unquestionably the best choice, and the decision about what kind to get is similar to that about what size of objective and power of magnification the scope itself should have: It's a matter of strength and weight—how much of the one a hunter needs versus how much of the other he can carry without growing exhausted. Guides who aren't packing a rifle will sometimes take a rifle stock with a bipod attachment and mount a spotting scope to it, giving them a solid viewing platform that allows them to remain close to the ground *(stay low to stay steady)* and out of sight and a way of slinging the scope on their shoulder when they're walking. (The solid support of a tripod or the like does much to compensate for the generally small exit pupil found on most spotting scopes when set at their highest power—what would appear as a revolving keyhole, if handheld, becomes a fixed image when standing on three legs.)

Beyond the sorts of support systems such as the ones described earlier, there really isn't much that's worth a damn. Hiking staffs may have wooden knobs at the top that can be

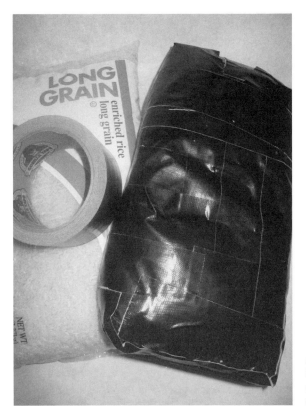

A support for a hunter's optics doesn't have to be complicated.

removed to reveal a screw threaded to accept the mounting hole of a camera or scope, creating a monopod. Monopods may work for photography, where the optical device needs to be held steady for only a fraction of a second, but they are almost always too unsteady for extended periods of viewing. A very simple supporting device is a "steady bag," and the simplest can be made from a five-pound bag of rice and a roll of duct tape. Put the steady bag on a rock, and the scope on the steady bag. Worse comes to worst in the field, a hunter can live off his steady bag for quite some time.

With whatever support a spotting scope may have, the key is to keep it as low to the ground as possible. Optically modern collapsible telescopes, one type of which is manufactured by Swarovski Optik, are available; and there are techniques for achieving a steady image through optics like these without a tripod: In the Highlands of Scotland, a *ghillie,* as the red-deer "stalking" guides in their tweed caps are known, will almost

Ghillie showing proper technique for viewing through a telescope in the field.

always have a traditional collapsible spotting scope in a leather case; assuming a comfortable and solid supine position in the heather, he will rest the extended telescope's objective on his crossed leg or braced against the shepherd's crook he uses for a walking staff, and sight the *hyne awa wee staggie*.

Spotting scopes may come with straight or angled tubes. There are compelling arguments for choosing either of these, though those arguments seem to boil down to how fast one can pick up an object when viewing with the scope mounted on the window of a truck. For that use, a straight-tube spotting scope is considered the better choice, though the advantage is minor. For overall viewing, an angled scope is probably superior. Remember again that the lower the scope, the steadier the image, and an angled tube allows for setting the scope lower. It is also

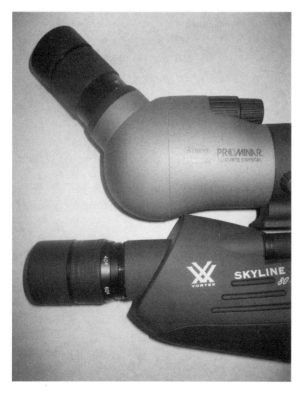

Spotting scopes come with angled (top) or straight (bottom) eyepieces.

a more comfortable position for extended periods of viewing to be sitting over an eyepiece and looking down through it, rather than having to crane one's neck upward to look through a straight-tube scope.

These matters are never without a "but," though; and there are hunters who prefer a straight tube over an angled one because while it may not lower the scope, it lowers the outline of a hunters body. Spotting scopes invariably come into play on the game with the most acute eyesight; so every advantage a hunter can take in concealing himself is worthwhile.

Speaking of viewing from a vehicle window, it is best not to take the righteous attitude that one would never stoop to such behavior that smacks of some sort of unsportsmanlike conduct. In fact, most hunters will probably do the greater percentage of their game viewing *(not hunting)* from a bucket seat, so there is no reason not to invest in a window mount of a quality commensurate with that of the optics to be affixed to it.

Another feature to which attention should be paid is the scope's focus mechanism. This mechanism is usually one of three types:

- There is the single drive knob on the top of the scope for coarse and fine focus. This type is considered by optics reviewers as "slow but precise," though it is not as conducive for achieving those absolutely crisp edges as other designs.
- Then there are two drive knobs, one coarse and the other fine. The coarse knob will generally be faster than a single knob at bringing an object into reasonable focus, and the fine knob provides those crystal-clear images—as always, assuming the knobs are focusing top-quality lenses.
- The third type of focus mechanism is known as "helical" and is a wide ring encircling the barrel of the scope. This allows for a quick switch between close and distant focus.

In comparing one with another, a hunter should consider the conditions under which he will be using the scope: Will he, for instance, be in cold weather, wearing thick gloves, making the manipulation of small knobs more difficult? (As for the actual process of bringing an object into focus, a hunter should adjust the focusing mechanism past the point where the image goes from sharp focus to slightly blurred, *then carefully return the image to the sharpest focus.*)

Other features to look for in a good spotting scope are an extendable sunshade for the objective to cut down on stray light and *baffling* (which will be discussed in more detail in the next chapter on the binocular, in which the procedure for evaluating optics in a store prior to purchase will also be discussed) to prevent internal reflections. A variable eyepiece will be more versatile than a straight-power one and should be of the *bayonet,* rather than the threaded, type for easy and positive attachment and removal. *Eyecups* need to be of the fold-in, screw-in, or push-pull design in order for eyeglass wearers to enjoy a full field of view. And look for lens caps that remain attached to the scope by lanyards or straps of some kind.

The $2,000 gorilla in the room is, finally: cost. There are a number of modestly priced (meaning just around a thousand bucks) spotting scopes that can provide years of dependable service, while a top-quality, top-price scope may provide a lifetime's usage. There is simply no one rule for what is too much or too little to pay for a really good spotting scope, just as there is no one way to say, ahead of its use in the field, what is too large and too heavy. An evaluation based on all the features and values examined in this chapter should, though, make it possible to arrive at a reasonably intelligent decision. If it ultimately comes down to picking *the* spotting scope from two likely candidates, then go with the smaller one in terms of objective size, power, weight, and price. Aided by the knowledge that he may always upgrade, a hunter can almost invariably make do with a little less scope rather than be shackled to a white elephant of which he can never rid himself.

SIDELIGHT:

The accepted wisdom is that Galileo was condemned by the Church of Rome for daring to espouse heliocentrism—the concept that the sun is the center of the universe around which all planets, including the Earth, revolve. The notion of heliocentrism goes back well before Galileo to at least seventh-century BC India and was for many centuries one of many hypotheses offered to explain the celestial phenomena observed by astronomers. An Earth-centric hypothesis was another of the explanations and was endorsed by both Ptolemy and before him Aristotle.

The purposes of science up to and during the time of Galileo were far different from what they are today, and it was not thought that scientific conclusions were to be taken as absolute accounts of reality. No one, therefore, would contend that any hypothesis for the workings of the universe was anything more than a hypothesis until the Polish polymath Nicolas Copernicus—a mathematician, economist, physician, jurist, administrator, governor, diplomat, military leader, scholar of the classics, Catholic priest and canon of Frombork cathedral, and astronomer—began formulating his theory of heliocentrism in the early 1500s and came to believe in it as a matter of scientific fact. In the 1530s he started circulating his ideas among other European scholars, who welcomed them with great excitement. Finally, in 1543, shortly before his death, he published, at the urging of a Catholic cardinal, his theory under the title *De revolutionibus orbium coelestium (On the Revolution of the Celestial Orbs)*.

Galileo and his telescope were able to verify Copernican theory. There is a certain kind of scientist, though, who believes that his expertise in one field automatically confers upon him a like expertise in another. Recent examples would be the late Nobel physicist William Shockley, who believed he was qualified to speak on eugenics, or linguist Noam Chomsky, who considers himself especially enlightened about foreign policy. Galileo, rather than leaving his discoveries to stand on their own, campaigned zealously through the 1610s to have the public accept Copernicanism as the "inconvenient truth" of his day, although many of his own theories concerning heliocentrism, beyond his telescopic observations, were incorrect—that the orbits of the planets, for instance, are perfectly circular or that tides are sloshed around by the Earth's rotation rather than by the pull of the moon's gravity—and were argued against, correctly, by fellow scientists of the time. This scientific squabbling and assorted attacks by ignorant, crackpot, and conniving monks and priests compelled Pope Paul V to turn the Galileo matter over to the Holy Office, i.e., the Inquisition, in Rome. Galileo's first trial, in 1616, ended in a relatively mild decree against him that did not include the word *heresy*.

There was, though, a mysterious document added to his file in the Holy Office, dated February 26, 1616, stating that Galileo would not be allowed to teach or discuss Copernicanism any longer. This document may have been forged, and in any case Galileo appears to have been unaware of it when in 1632 he wrote *Dialogue on the Two Great World Systems,* both a discussion of heliocentrism and a scathing satire directed at the defenders of the Ptolemaic view of the universe, including in a vaguely disguised persona his friend and supporter Pope Urban VIII. This led to Galileo's second trial in 1633, a pro-forma but empty threat of torture, and his condemnation as being "vehemently suspected of heresy." His sentence amounted to his remaining silent on Copernicus and under house arrest in his country villa near Florence, where he died in bed at age seventy-seven.

Since Galileo, the church has been unjustly accused of being opposed to scientific study, even though heliocentrism was never heresy under Catholic dogma, and in 1741 the Holy Office granted *imprimatur* ("let it be printed") to all of Galileo's works. In 1822 the work of Canon Settele, putting forth Copernicanism as physical fact, also received imprimatur. In 1979 Pope John Paul II asked the Pontifical Academy of Sciences to examine Galileo's trials, and in 1992 the conclusion was reached that the scientist had been unjustly condemned. And Galileo, to the best of known historical fact, never dropped anything off the Tower of Pisa.

THE BINOCULAR ▮4▮

The word *binoculars* makes as much sense as a singular noun as would *a bicycles* or *a bipeds*. A "binocular" is two linked telescopes with two oculars, or eyepieces. In other words, binocular means "two eyepieces" in just the same way that *bicycle* means "two wheels."

Another definition of binocular would simply be "the most essential optical device that any hunter can carry." Spotting scopes, as it is hoped has been shown, are extremely useful in the field; and the riflescope, to be discussed in the next chapter, can be thought of as the "queen of optics," as the bayonet was considered the "queen of weapons" to the *chasseur*-trousered Zouaves of the Civil War. Nonetheless, many a head of game have been taken without first being sighted through a spotting scope, and more than a few successful shots have been made with iron sights. It is difficult, though, to imagine any hunting situation in which a binocular would not come into play.

The binocular is the most essential piece of optical equipment a hunter can carry in the field. This hunter is also showing a good position for steady glassing.

It might almost be said that the binocular is the perfect optical device because it mirrors human binocular vision and depth perception. The very first thought after the telescope was developed, or perhaps simultaneous with it, was to turn that device into a binocular viewing instrument. Almost immediately upon Lippershey's application for a patent on his *kijkglas* in 1608, he was asked by the patent authorities to produce a binocular device, which he did within weeks. It was virtually self-evident that any optical instrument that lets you look through it with both eyes open is going to be superior to anything that makes you squint through it with only one.

Throughout the seventeenth and eighteenth centuries binoculars based on the Galilean telescope continued to be manufactured, and in fact this was the design of numerous cheap binoculars well into the twentieth century. Such binoculars were more often called by the self-defining name of "field glasses." Field glasses were not capable of magnification of much over 5X. The Keplerian design could have provided higher power, but there was the problem of the inverted image, although by the nineteenth century erector systems made with two spaced lenses were in use in terrestrial, rather than astronomical, telescopes; and it's presumed they were also to be found in some field glasses.

The man who made possible the modern binocular, as opposed to field glasses, was Ignazio Porro. Porro (1801–1875) was an artillery officer and surveyor in the Italian army. After retiring from military service in his early forties, Porro opened an optical workshop in Turin and later moved to Paris. It was there that he developed his most famous device, the reflective prism.

A *prism* is, classically, a solid-glass body with three parallelogram faces on the sides and triangular ends that refracts white light so that it separates into its spectrum of colors—red, orange, yellow, green, blue, indigo, and violet, remembered by the acronym "Roy G. Biv." This is known as a *dispersive prism* for its dispersion of light. The prism for which Porro is known is the reflective prism he patented in 1854. This prism, which resembles a toppled-over roof, changes the direction in which the light is traveling by 180 degrees and is eponymously named a *Porro prism*. When two such prisms are arranged "orthogonally"—at right angles to each other—this is called a "double Porro prism" (essentially paired roof prisms) and was another of *signore* Porro's patents. He utilized these prisms mainly in telescopes (which is more ironic than it may sound, as shall be seen) and presented a pair of his handiworks to France's last monarch, Emperor Napoléon III. Porro's inventions brought him little business success, and he was much maligned by the French scientific community, his being Italian probably not to his benefit. He returned to Italy to teach and open other workshops; but at the time of his death he was in near penury, virtually unknown and had little faith in his being remembered for any of the work he had done.

Porro was almost right. In 1893 when the German mathematician and physicist Ernst Abbe sought a patent for his own double roof prisms, with both elements cemented together, he learned to his surprise that the basic design was already patented. Abbe (1840–1905) came from an impoverished background in which he had watched his father work sixteen-hour days. Abbe was able to make his way through college on scholarships and became a member of the faculty of the university in Jena, where he met the optics manufacturer Carl Zeiss in 1866.

Zeiss (1816–1888) had opened an optics shop in 1846 in Jena *(pronounced "YAY-na")* to manufacture microscopes—another Dutch invention in which the seeming omnipresent Lippershey may have played a role and for which the seventeenth-century Delft drapery merchant and scientist Thonius Philips van Leeuwenhoek (pronounced *vahn Laywenhook*) had discovered an

Modern-day Zeiss lenses and prisms.

innovative method of producing tiny glass spheres for use as high-quality lenses in his microscopes, making it possible for him to view bacteria, which he called "animalcules." Within twenty years Zeiss had sold one thousand of his microscopes, a not insignificant number for such precision instruments. After joining up with Zeiss, Abbe formulated many theoretical and practical advancements in lens making and would state that Zeiss lenses were made according to exact computations, "so that any trial-and-error approach is eliminated."

The main impediment to fine optics was still the quality of the glass. When Lippershey made those binoculars, the patent office insisted that he use quartz crystals for the lenses—much more temperamental than glass to grind but able to render far better clarity. Three hundred years later optical glass was apparently not a great deal better. The high degree of resolution that Abbe's calculations said was possible could not be achieved with the glass that was available. Glass could not be made homogenous enough and caused light rays to bend erratically due to the variability of the indices of refraction inside the glass.

Then Zeiss and Abbe met Otto Schott (1851–1935), at the time a thirty-year-old with a doctorate in chemistry, specializing in the properties of glass. Collaborating with Abbe, Schott developed what we now know as "apochromatic"glass *(see Chapter 3 for discussion of "apochromatic" glass)*, to which Abbe's formulae could be fully applied. Apochromatic lenses became the objectives of Zeiss's finest microscopes, Zeiss himself contributing a technique for making eyepieces for the instruments that practically eliminated color fringing.

After the death of his friend Carl in 1888, Abbe took control of the Zeiss company. In 1889 he founded the Carl-Zeiss-Stiftung (the Carl Zeiss Foundation), which became sole owner of the company in 1891. Meanwhile Zeiss expanded its line to include photographic lenses and terrestrial telescopes and, despite having

Early Zeiss
Porro-prism
binocular.
Photo
courtesy of
Carl Zeiss, Inc.

been beaten to it by almost forty years, a Porro-prism—actually a Porro-Abbe prism—binocular in 1894. This was the first truly high-quality modern binocular and is still admired by connoisseurs of fine optics for its sharpness and attractive design. Abbe was also an innovator when it came to labor relations. Recalling his father's ceaseless toil, he instituted an eight-hour workday at Zeiss and offered employees such previously unheard-of benefits as paid holidays, sick pay, and pensions.

Before traveling any farther along in the history of the binocular, this might be an appropriate place to discuss the difference between the *Porro-prism* (as it is generally known) and the *roof-prism* binocular. In a Porro-prism binocular, light enters through the objective and travels into the prism, where it strikes four reflective surfaces, makes four 90-degree turns, is erected, and finally sent out the eyepiece. This lets the ocular be offset inward from the aperture but also allows the light to travel a longer distance than simply the length or height of the instrument and helps create a wider angular magnification and better

The roof-prism binocular, left, and the Porro-prism, right.

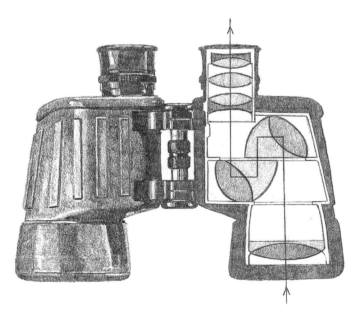

Diagram of a Porro-prism binocular

Diagram of a roof-prism binocular.

image at the ocular. It also makes for a somewhat larger and heavier binocular than one with a roof prism.

The irony is, again, that a single Porro prism is a roof prism; but the roof prisms used in binoculars today, even though their individual elements may share the Porro's essential rooflike shape, are usually labeled "Abbe-Koenig" or "Schmidt-Pechan." Of the two, the Abbe-Koenig is the choice for long, slim binoculars such as a 7x42-millimeter, while the Schmidt-Pechan (or simply "Pechan") seems best suited for pocket-sized binoculars. In any roof prism the image enters and emerges along the same direct path, though while inside the prism it is reflected into a number of turns of various degrees and is erected, as it is through a Porro prism. But the straight line of flight, or line of light, through a roof prism allows the ocular and the aperture of the binocular tube to be in alignment; this, plus the prism's more compact size in comparison with a Porro, makes for a trimmer profile and a lighter instrument.

For many years after both types of binoculars were available, the Porro prism was considered optically superior in both depth of field and in producing the look of three dimensions. A roof prism was thought difficult to grind to top quality; and the light, in a prism such as a Schmidt-Pechan, was reflected more times, and so more of it could be lost by straying off or being absorbed by the glass. Today, though, with the vast improvements in glass, grinding techniques, and coatings (including what is known as *phase coating* in roof prisms to correct different light waves' being out of phase with one another and so causing a degradation in resolution and contrast—more apparent at higher powers of magnification, this fault might be thought of as a timing problem in light transmission, like a timing problem in a car's engine), in short with all of the above, there is very little, if any, optical difference between the Porro-prism and the roof-prism binocular. However, the popularity (or marketing) of the roof-prism binocular is such that the Porro is slowly fading from the product catalogs of serious optics makers.[v]

For at least the early part of the twentieth century, European manufacturers dominated the market in quality binoculars. Zeiss, to be sure, was the big dog on the block; but following relatively closely behind was Leitz, the forerunner of Leica (the name "Leica" is a combination of *Leitz* and *ca*mera). The origins of Leitz, and Leica extend back to the Hessian mechanic and autodidactic mathematician Carl Kellner (1826–1855). In 1849 Kellner founded in Wetzlar, Germany, the Optical Institute, which would ultimately evolve into Leica. Kellner helped refine the achromatic lens; after his untimely death, his widow, Belthle, assumed control of his company.

In 1864 another precision optical mechanic, Ernst Leitz, joined the firm and later became a partner and finally took over the concern in 1869 after the death of Belthle. He renamed the enterprise "Ernst Leitz GmbH" (for those who have always been curious, "GmbH" stands for *Gesellschaft mit beschränkter Haftung,* which translated literally means a "company with limited liability"), which expanded rapidly with the popularity of its binocular microscopes. In 1907 Leitz entered into the manufacture of field binoculars.

A story associated with Leitz and little known till recent years concerns Ernst's son, Ernst II, who assumed control of the company after his father's death, and Ernst II's daughter, Elsie Kuhn-Leitz. With Hitler's ascendancy to power in Germany in 1933 and the passage of the 1935 Nuremberg laws restricting the rights of Jews to work and travel, Jewish friends, associates, and employees of Leitz began seeking help in leaving the country. Leitz responded by making these people and their families, and even their friends, paper sales associates of the company, paying them small stipends and assigning them to Leitz offices outside the country. These "salespersons" began appearing in Britain, France, even Hong Kong. Those who reached the United States were found jobs in the photographic industry through the Leitz Manhattan office. This enterprise became known as the "Leitz Freedom Train" and reached its height in 1938–39. Members of the Leitz family escaped severe punishment by the Reich because they were not Jewish and because of the vital importance of their products to the Wehrmacht. Nonetheless, Elsie was arrested at the Swiss border as she was helping a Jewish woman escape from the country and endured a harsh interrogation at the hands of the Gestapo before being released. The Leitz Freedom Train remained a secret for half a century or more until the deaths of all the family members who had participated in it.

During the early decades of the twentieth century, the binocular market was dominated by the Germans, but the shape of things to come began to coalesce in the 1920s when German engineers employed by Nippon Kogaku ("Japan Optics"), formed in 1917 by the merger of three Japanese optical companies, advised the company in the development of a line of pocket prism binoculars. The company went on to manufacture camera lenses, then cameras and spotting scopes and riflescopes and in 1988 adopted the name "Nikon Corporation."

In 1862 Daniel Swarovski was born in the northern Bohemian town of Jiřetín pod Bukovou, which would become part of the Habsburg Empire and is now in the Czech Republic. He was a glass cutter and jeweler, and in 1892 he patented an electric cutting machine for the production of a type of lead-crystal glass known as *das Geschmeide*. In 1895 he founded his own company and moved his operations to the Austrian Tyrol town of Wattens, where the waters of the eastern Alps provided the hydroelectric power for his cutting machines. In 1935 his eldest son, Wilhelm, produced a prototype for a binocular, which naturally came to the Wehrmacht's attention. Thus diverted by the war, the Swarovski Optik brand of Habicht ("Hawk") binoculars and other optics did not reach the public until 1949.

The origins of the Asahi Optical Corporation can be traced to a shop that produced eyeglass lenses, founded in 1919 by Kumao Kajiwara in the Tokyo suburb of Toshima. The company soon expanded into the field of lenses for motion-picture and still cameras and predictably was drawn into the imperial war effort. In 1948, during General Douglas MacArthur's proconsulship in Japan, Asahi stole a page from Nikon and came out with a line of miniature binoculars with coated lenses and the trade name of "Jupiter." Despite all the lenses produced for the cameras of many other makers, it was not until 1950 that the company made a camera of its own and in 1957 introduced the first Japanese pentaprism single-lens-reflex camera called "Pentax," the name by which the company is best known today.

And what of American binocular makers during this time? There were apparently not many, at least none of any notably high quality or size of production. Extremely fine lenses had been crafted since the 1800s by the German-founded company of Bausch and Lomb in Rochester, New York, but these ended up being used in other, many of them foreign, manufacturers' binoculars and optical devices. As in Europe and Japan, any binocular that might have been produced by American optical companies during World War II went directly to the U.S. military rather than to the civilian market.

In 1913 David Pearsall Bushnell was born in St. Paul, Minnesota, and grew up in Los Angeles. At sixteen he bought a new Chevrolet with cash he had earned by selling newspapers and went on selling newspapers to pay his tuition at the California Institute of Technology. After Cal Tech he hitchhiked to New York with plans to sail around the world on a tramp steamer but ended up in Europe for eight months until all his savings were exhausted.

Back in the United States, Bushnell enrolled in the University of Southern California and earned a bachelor's degree in foreign commerce. When World War II began, he got a job with Lockheed Aircraft and stayed four years. After the war he started an export business and in 1947 took the job of delivering steel reinforcing bars, made from the rails of L.A.'s defunct Pacific Electric streetcar system, to Hong Kong. Before he set sail on his first trans-Pacific business trip, he thought he should be a proper tourist and have a binocular to hang around his neck. The only one he could find was in a pawn shop, a 6x30-millimeter made by Universal Camera in Minneapolis. He paid $50, and when his ship reached Manila Bay, someone on the dock saw him looking through the binocular and offered him $100 for it. It was Bushnell's first optics sale.

From Hong Kong, Bushnell decided to fulfill his earlier wish to travel around the world and went to Shanghai, where a Dutch trader showed him an attractive 7x50-millimeter binocular the Dutchman had just picked up in Tokyo as a sales sample, having paid $18 for it. Bushnell obtained a permit to travel to occupied Japan as soon as possible—this was late 1947—and acquired sample binoculars at an export exhibition, shipped them back to his office in Pasadena, California, and continued on to Bangkok, Germany, and London, carrying an Asahi 6x15-millimeter binocular.

Back home he found that he had four hundred orders for binoculars from retailers, so he imported the 6x15s from Asahi. A shipping strike tied up the binoculars at the dock until after the 1948 Christmas season, and afterward the shop owners cancelled their orders and remained leery of the "Made in Japan" stamp on Bushnell's merchandise, believing that German and other European binoculars would soon be returning to the American market. Luckily for Bushnell, Santa Anita's winter horseracing season was just opening, and his Asahi binoculars proved perfect for the railbirds.

After that, Bushnell began making mail-order sales through ads he placed in magazines such as *Sports Afield*. He then started putting his name on the products he imported and became a full-fledged optics company. He saw Bushnell Performance Optics grow into the largest source of binoculars in the country and in 1972 sold his company to Bausch and Lomb. In the late 1970s, when he and his wife visited the widow of his old trading partner Saburo Matsumoto, the CEO of Asahi, Mrs. Matsumoto told him about all the times when what she and her husband ate for dinner depended on the size of the order they had received from Bushnell that day. Bushnell died in 2005.

After this admittedly incomplete and utterly imperfect history of the development of the binocular and how it has found its way into the hands of hunters, three broad considerations remain. These are the acquiring, the employing, and the carrying of the binocular:

ACQUIRING:

Whether a binocular is purchased new or used, traded for, or passed along, there are several factors to be examined in order to determine an instrument's worth (not necessarily its monetary value) for viewing in the field.

What to look for when acquiring a binocular:

- Price: Although acquiring a good binocular is not all about the Benjamins, it really is the first place to start. Many guidebooks on how to buy optics discuss the "cost" of them, but none ever seems to talk about the "price." A binocular can run the gamut from inexpensive to "Holy . . .!" but that does nothing to explain the price tag it carries. In fact, any one make and model of binocular can have as many as four different and competing prices—and this same pattern of pricing applies to all other optics as well.

  The first price is the *MSRP* ("manufacturer's suggested retail price"). This is the price that the maker publishes—often in product literature—and at which the maker believes, or says, the binocular should be sold. This price exists to allow retailers to show consumers how much of a bargain the retailers are offering with their own price compared with the maker's. No one should ever, under any circumstances, eat in a place called "Grandma's," bet on a horse with bandages, or pay MSRP.

  MAP ("minimum advertised price") is second, and it is a figure approved by the manufacturer that retailers may show in their published or broadcast advertising. Obviously

MAP will be less than MSRP, sometimes considerably. Its function is to enable smaller shop owners to compete with the big-box stores, which could always undercut the "little guy" if permitted to blazon "low-low prices" set at a level so far beneath the floor established by the MAP that small-volume retailers could never hope to receive a decent return from their far fewer number of sales.

Next comes the *real world price*. In case that term is not self-explanatory enough, this is the average price a consumer can expect to pay when purchasing a binocular from a retailer, whether a shop, big-box store, or a catalog. This price will sometimes appear in printed reviews of a binocular, and it can fluctuate from retailer to retailer, depending on how much profit retailers hope to make. As a rule, though, it will not be too far from the MAP though can still be significantly different. To reiterate, a real world price below the MAP cannot be publicly advertised. A hunter has to walk into the store to find out what is actually written on the sticker.

The *Internet auction price* is a fourth possibility. It takes a certain amount of raw nerve to bid on a binocular at one of the auction sites, especially on a used one with a more expensive name, but very substantial savings may be found. Fine-quality binoculars have a lengthy shelf life, and ones made ten or even twenty years ago, although they may lack some of the more advanced antireflective coatings or newer glass—but as long as they have not been abused—can continue to function quite satisfactorily today. A hidden treasure to be on the lookout for is any really top-brand binocular that has been refurbished and carries a factory warranty. A binocular like this will be as good as new (and some think even better because if the binocular had a manufacturing defect, that defect ought to have been remedied by the factory), and at a price that ought to be well below what the binocular originally sold for, in current dollars.

One last consideration with regard to the price of a binocular is where that price should be paid. Leaving online auctions aside, the three choices are the small retailer, the big-box store, and a catalog. The first will almost always have the highest price, although there could be times when he is selling off, at an extremely attractive price, old stock that has long been gone from the other two outlets. The primary reason for purchasing from a small retailer, aside from an understandable desire to buy locally, is the hope that he will offer more insight into the quality of a binocular than can some guy in a vest stacking boxes with a forklift in a mammoth warehouse operation or the florid prose accompanying the grainy product photo in a catalog. That, and the promise of courteous after-sale service—both admittedly being about as likely as finding Keith Richards in rehab. Between the big box and the catalog, a hunter has to use time and gas to drive to the store; so even with shipping and handling, the catalog price may be less. One thing that hunters cannot do, though, when they buy a binocular through a catalog is to inspect it physically to see how well it "fits" them, an aspect of the buying experience that cannot be discounted (see "What a Brochure Can't Tell a Hunter" following).

When the question of price is understood, then the issue of a binocular's cost—what a hunter is getting in exchange for the price he pays—can be balanced against the features that binocular offers, with many of the same features being applicable to the other types of hunting optics.

- **Glass:** The alpha and omega of any binocular. A binocular can be thought of as nothing more than a convenient way of carrying around a lot of glass lenses and keeping them aligned and in focus. Considerations such as low-dispersion and antireflective coatings have already been discussed in previous chapters, so the only other matter to consider is that the better the optical glass, the more it is likely to weigh, and so the more it can add to the overall weight of the binocular (although much of the best optical glass of late, because it no longer contains lead due to environmental considerations, is also less heavy).

- **Light Transmission:** Exit pupil, twilight factor, depth of field, and relative brightness have been previously explained *(see also footnote iii)*. An important question, though, is how much light actually passes through the optical system of a binocular and reaches a hunter's eye? This is a figure that can make for delightfully entertaining bedtime reading in binocular advertising brochures. Some manufacturers will underscore the fact that the layer of antireflective coating they apply will permit something like "99.8 percent" of the available light to pass through, which may be perfectly true. Yet, what they often fail to mention is how many layers of coating are applied to each surface, how many air-to-glass surfaces are contained in their binocular (light loss being multiplied with each of those surfaces), and that a 0.2 percent loss of light is probably a reference to what is lost by the *best* (and most costly) layer of antireflective coating being used and not for all the other (cheaper) ones put on in order to call the lenses "multicoated" without being accused of false advertising, at least within the letter of the law. A relevant number is the percentage of the available light that travels through the objective and the entire optical system and exits from the ocular. If a binocular manufacturer can guarantee anywhere from 90 to 92 percent transmission of light through the binocular, that is about as good as it gets. *The law of physics, for its part, guarantees that the amount of light coming out of any optical device—other than night-vision optics—will be less than the amount that went in. It is not only impossible for any binocular to "gather" more light than what is available but also impossible for it to gather as* much. *If an image appears brighter through a binocular (or spotting scope or riflescope) than without it, that is a textbook example of* trompe l'oeil, *not to mention* trompe la cervelle, "to trick the brain." *We see what we want to see, even through a glass, darkly.*

- **IPD:** *Interpupillary distance* is a term for describing how far apart someone's pupils are. For most adults this is between 58 and 72 millimeters; most binoculars can be adjusted within this range so that the eyepieces are the right distance apart in order for the centers of the eyes to coincide with the centers of the eyepieces, creating a single round sight picture rather than two overlapping ones. Some individuals can, though, have extremely narrow- or extremely wide-set eyes. If a hunter believes he fits into one of those categories, then he does need to try a binocular before buying it to determine if it can be adjusted to the proper degree of spread. One of the several virtues of the Porro-prism binocular over the roof prism is that it can in general offer a more generous range of hinge adjustments.

- **Eye Relief:** This is, lamentably, not another way of saying "Scarlett Johansson." It is the distance that the eyepiece may be held away from the eye and still provide the viewer with the complete field of view *(see "Field of View" following)* instead of a kind of tunnel vision. This distance can fall into a range that is sometimes called the "eye box."

Some binoculars may have a very small eye box of 9 to 14 millimeters, which might be comfortable for most people who do not wear eyeglasses. For glasses wearers, though, or for those who took to heart the earlier message in the book about always wearing eye protection and want to keep their protective glasses on in the field, it is estimated that an eye relief of at least 16 millimeters is required to see the whole picture. If that is something that cannot be ascertained by reading the technical data about a binocular, then a hunter needs, again, to get a hold of an actual sample in a store and put it to his eyes to find out if it will give him the relief he seeks.

- **Eyecups:** These are the soft rings around the eyepieces that determine where a hunter places his eyes. These can be adjusted in several ways, depending on how they are manufactured. Some simply fold out or in to suit those with glasses and those without, or the eyecups can push in or pull out, or turn in or turn out. In the first instance, the synthetic rubber of the eyecup can fatigue and crack in time from the folding as well as from plain age. Better binoculars seem to use one of the latter two systems. Ideally a hunter would like to feel how the eyecups extend and retract to know that they are tight but smooth and will stay reliably locked in position and are not shaky to the touch.

- **Field of View:** Field of view ("FOV") can be described as "true" or "apparent." True field of view is the angle subtended *(see discussion of "subtension" in Chapter 3)* by the objective lens. An 8.5x43-millimeter binocular may have a true (or at least published) field of view of 6.1 degrees. This is the wedge, or cone, of light entering the objective. Thought of simply as width, this is how wide an area from which the objective is drawing light and accordingly is the physical width, or diameter, of the area that may be observed. The formula for determining this in feet is:

52.5 X FOV in degrees = FOV in feet @ 1,000 yards

So for the binocular described earlier, its FOV in feet at 1,000 yards would be:

52.5 X 6.1° = 320.25 feet @ 1,000 yards

As the light passes through the eyepiece, the angle is widened. This is the apparent field of view (called "AFOV" for convenience). Somewhat tougher to comprehend, AFOV is calculated by multiplying the degrees of true FOV by the magnification power. Thus, for the binocular mentioned earlier:

6.1° X 8.5 power = AFOV of 51.85°

As was stated previously, a magnified image *"is not made larger; it is brought closer—through the widening of the arc it subtends and the greater area of the retina it covers."* Put another way, the image comes out of the eyepiece in a larger angle than it entered through the objective. The image remains the same width in feet; but the binocular has brought it, virtually, 8.5 times closer to us, causing it to widen 8.5 times in our vision and therefore to take up or occupy 8.5 times more of our visual field (51.85 degrees versus 6.1 degrees).

As a practical consideration, a hunter has to weigh the advantages of a binocular with a wider FOV against the disadvantages. A binocular may have a FOV of between approximately 5 and 10 degrees, and all things being equal, such as the diameter of the objective, the FOV will narrow as magnification power rises. Some binoculars, though, represent themselves as "wide angle." These can be fine for maintaining a view of fast-moving animals—a herd of pronghorn antelope running over the plains like a flock of birds skimming the yellow grass. There comes a point, though, where distortion will begin to creep into a wide angle, especially at the edges of the image, decreasing its useful and esthetic value. An ideal image should demonstrate perfect *flatness of field,* meaning that the image remains equally sharp from its center to its farthest periphery.

- **Focus Mechanism:** This can actually be more of an issue than might first be assumed. The three types are *fixed-focus, individual eyepiece focusing* ("IF"), and *center-focus.* A hunter should just put the first one right out of his mind. A fixed-focus binocular assumes that a user has both perfect vision and vision that is perfectly matched in both eyes and that those eyes are young and flexible enough to do a great deal of accommodating before a hammer of Thor eyestrain headache takes hold. "Fixed focus" fairly screams "shoddy!"

    An IF binocular can adjust for the vision in each eye; but once that is accomplished, it is fundamentally the same as a fixed-focus. Images at varying distances may be in focus, but this will be the result of unconscious accommodation and will bring on eventual visual weariness. A good center-focus binocular is always the best choice, assuming it has on one of the eyepieces an individual *dioptric adjustment (see "Keeping It Sharp" below)* that will enable it to be properly focused for each of the viewer's eyes and can then be refocused as required for objects at different ranges through the use of the central drive wheel.

A center-focus wheel at the bottom of the binocular's hinge is more "hunter friendly."

One of the "small" touches that a hunter wants to look at in a hunting binocular is the location of the center-focus wheel. Most binoculars place it at the top of the hinge. This is fine, but for best use in the field, the wheel by all rights ought to be at the bottom. If at the top, the wheel will be under the brim of a hunter's cap, making it necessary for him to tip it back in order to adjust the focus on an animal or other object. Without fail, the wind will come up and blow the cap off his head every time he has to change focus. It also makes it nearly impossible to focus while squeezing down on the cap brim to help lock the binocular in place *(see "Keeping It Steady" following)*. A focus wheel at the bottom of the hinge will eliminate all these problems, if only more manufacturers understood enough about the needs of hunters to build their binoculars that way.

- **Housing:** Some manufacturers are downright effusive about their binocular's "polymer" housing—as if they were Martha Stewart and this was a good thing. And perhaps it is. In time, no doubt, all binoculars and other optics will have housings, not to mention lenses, of *plastic,* and hunters will probably wonder how they could have lived so long without them. For now, though, quality binocular housings continue to be made of metal. When they were known as "field glasses" rather than "binoculars," that metal was brass; but now it may be magnesium or what is invariably described as "aircraft grade" aluminum or even titanium. The goal is to use a metal that can be both strong and light. For optimum use by a hunter, the housing should also be rubber armored to protect it and to reduce any alarm-inducing metallic clangs that might be produced by a branch or the like hitting the binocular as a hunter is closing in on those last few yards to get into shooting position on a 7x7 bull elk.

- **Waterproof and Fogproof:** Hunting can be a far-from-fair-weather pursuit, so hunting optics must be able to stand up to the elements. A hunting binocular must be both *waterproof* and *fogproof.* "Waterproof" ought to be clear, and the technical data for a binocular will guarantee that it will remain free of any leakage when submerged to a particular depth, such as "down to five meters." The integrity of a guarantee of waterproofness can be tested by dunking a binocular into a tub of water and holding it under while the hunter checks for streams of small bubbles emerging from the housing. (Stray air may be trapped around the housing when it is first submerged, and bubbles from this will be few, erratic, and larger, unlike the steady column of tiny champagne-like bubbles that represents a leak in the internal seals that is allowing the purging gas to escape.) "Fogproof" guarantees that the binocular, if subject to sharp changes in temperature, will not have condensation form within it; condensation is also capable of leading to corrosion. Fogproofing is obtained by replacing all the atmospheric air and any attendant moisture that may have entered a binocular on dust during the assembly process with the pure, dry, nearly inert gas nitrogen or the even less reactive "noble gas" argon. Some manufacturers claim that argon is superior to nitrogen because even as a monatomic gas, as opposed to diatomic nitrogen, argon is much larger and so will escape (and all purging gases, over time, will escape) more slowly from the binocular housing than will nitrogen, maintaining fogproofing better and longer.

Field & Stream icon
David Petzal
checks binoculars
for waterproofness.

- **What a Brochure Can't Tell a Hunter:** Some individual qualities of a binocular can be judged only when that binocular is in a hunter's hands, and that means picking one up and messing about with it. If a hunter enters a shop and asks to take a look at a particular binocular, the person behind the counter will obligingly hand it to him and invite him to step outside to have a look through it. This will tell a hunter almost exactly as much about that binocular as taking a test drive in "Park" would tell him about a new pickup. All but the worst possible binoculars will look good, or at least passing, when used in broad daylight. A hunter will be much better off to stay inside and focus the binocular on something on the shop's far wall, something with small print on it, to gauge its *resolution*—its ability to bring fine detail into sharp focus.

  The most accurate way of judging the resolution of a binocular is to view the 1951 United States Air Force Resolution Test Target through it. The 1951 Chart is to optics what the Snellen Chart on the opthalmologist's wall is to human vision. Instead of being made up of a big "E" and clusters of progressively smaller letters, as the Snellen Chart is, the 1951 Target—which usually comes mounted on a three-inch-square glass plate—is comprised of groups of three bars that descend in size to the nearly imperceptible. The smaller the lines that can be seen clearly, the finer the binocular's resolution; but checking a binocular against a resolution target is not something a hunter can do in a store—and probably not something he will do at home, either. Instead, when buying a binocular a hunter should try reading a product label at 30 feet by the indoor light of the store. It's not as precise a method as the test target, but it is still a fair yardstick for evaluating optical quality before putting down a credit card. (It is also a good way of gauging an optical device's close-focus range.)

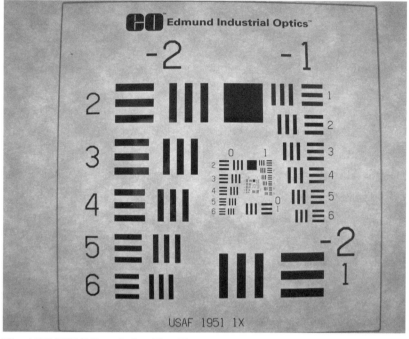

The 1951 USAF Resolution Test Target.

A binocular brochure may or may not specify the type of glass that is used for the prism, but usually it will be either BK-7 borosilicate flint glass or BaK-4 barium crown glass. There is no reason for this to mean anything to a hunter, except that BaK-4 is considered superior to BK-7. The difference between the two, though, is noticeable when a binocular is held out and pointed toward the light, and the exit pupil is examined. On a binocular with a BK-7 prism the exit pupil will be squared off and gray edged, while one with a BaK-4 prism will produce a clean, well-lighted exit pupil, one that is round and evenly illuminated.

Stray light is reflections off the internal surfaces of the binocular that can degrade the image the hunter sees through the eyepiece. The lens mounts, edges of the lenses themselves, or other places inside the housing can reflect stray light; a manufacturer of premium optics will take care to lessen or eliminate internal reflection by anodizing or painting bare metal and other shiny surfaces inside the housing, a process known as *baffling*. A hunter can check a binocular's baffling by looking for any loose gleams or reflections inside the housing while viewing a full, bright FOV—everything around the image should be flat black. (The quality of the baffling can be even better judged by looking through the binocular backward through the objective lens.)

One reason for carrying a binocular out of the shop into the daylight is to check for chromatic aberration *(see Chapter 3)*. A recommended method for doing this is to find a high-contrast image, such as a leafy tree, and place it in the center of the FOV against the sky. A hunter would then look for green or violet color fringing at the edges of the image. And as long as the hunter has the binocular in his hands, he can work the hinges and eyecups so he can decide what

Compare binoculars one against the other when evaluating quality.

he thinks about its overall construction while ruminating upon the weight, bulk, and shape of the binocular—how it *feels* to him personally. (This kind of testing works better when comparing two binoculars simultaneously. Stack one on top of the other on a steady rest, and compare the images produced by each.)

About the only other thing that a hunter *may* be able to tell by a hands-on/eyes-on examination of a binocular is its *collimation*. This is frequently defined as the alignment between the two barrels of the binocular—do they point and focus on the same target—but it can also refer to the way the lenses are stacked up with one another inside the housing. Only rather severe collimation defects, such as double images, would be immediately detectable during a brief viewing through a binocular, with more minor, though finally no less annoying ones probably becoming apparent only after the purchase and some extended use in the field. Collimation problems can appear in any binocular, no matter how precisely made, after enough time in service, which is another reason for a hunter to make certain that any piece of optics he purchases comes with a lifetime warranty, and that he reads the fine print closely before paying his money.

EMPLOYING:

Using a binocular would seem a clear-cut proposition, yet there are several steps that a hunter should follow in order to achieve the instrument's maximum potential. And so the following ought to be kept in mind:

- **Keeping It Sharp:** A hunter who does not bother to set up his binocular properly is like a chef who never whets his knife on a steel. A hunter should begin by opening the hinge so that the eyepieces are set at the correct interpupillary distance. It is then necessary to have the eyecups extended or retracted to the right position to provide the best eye relief and the greatest field of view, with or without eyeglasses. (If this bears echoes of "Ned in the first primer," the regrettable fact is that too many hunters simply do not pay enough attention to these fundamental steps before using their binoculars in the field.) To focus the binocular a hunter should (presuming he made the sound decision to go with the type of center-focus model described earlier) hold it as steadily as possible and look through the eyepiece without the dioptric adjustment. Closing his other eye, he will use the center-focus wheel to bring the image into sharp focus, following the method of going past the sharpest focus, then returning to it. The reverse adjustment should be made slowly until the image *just* comes into focus again. Then with that eye closed and the other—the one viewing through the eyepiece with the dioptric adjustment (usually the right one)—open, the dioptric focus ring is adjusted until that eyepiece is, similarly, focused. With both eyes open, the image should be a single sharp circle without any distortion. (Another quality of a binocular to examine is how well the dioptric lens stays in focus without drifting.)

- **Keeping It Steady:** In the field a hunter will, of course, not always have the luxury of having a tripod to mount his binocular on or of finding the most solid rest. There will be times when he has to snap his binocular up to have a chance of getting a look at some fleeting image. Those sort of heroic manly poses so often seen in the sporting gazettes, those of some granite-jawed Hawkeye holding his binocular in one mighty fist, represent a general waste of time when it comes to viewing much of anything. At a bare minimum,

A tripod is not always available for a binocular in the hunting field.

a hunter should endeavor always to use the two prehensile-thumbed hands that evolution was gracious enough to bequeath him when he is looking through his binocular.

When viewing, a hunter wants to keep his elbows tucked into his body to form a brace against which his forearms may rest. If he has to view while standing, a harness *(see following)* may help to keep the binocular steady, or he can try holding it into place by wrapping his fingers around the top of the bill of his cap, if he is wearing one, and using upward thumb pressure to sandwich the binocular against the bill's underside while pulling down on the bill with his fingers. This will create a "push me-pull you" locking tension like that of assuming a two-handed grip on a pistol in which the rear hand is pushing while the front one is pulling, holding everything steady—at least until muscle fatigue sets in.

Homo erectus makes for a fairly unstable viewing platform when it lacks any outside support. This is where it does become advantageous to have a good hiking staff. If it is the telescoping variety, it can be set at the right height at which to rest the binocular and also to let the hunter rest some of his own weight against it to dampen the swaying and tremor that is inherent in the human bipedal posture. A hunter should also look around for any immovable object, such as a tree or rock or fencepost, upon or against which he can rest his binocular. Still, viewing from any standing position is always going to be far inferior to getting as low to the ground as possible.

The steadiest viewing will be achieved by a hunter's lying prone with his elbows on the ground. (Placing the binocular on a daypack or rolled-up jacket, a fallen log, or that steady bag of rice the hunter remembered to bring along only improves image stability.) Second best, and providing more mobile viewing, is for a hunter to sit with his back resting firmly on something and his elbows braced against his knees. (Straddling an upright packframe creates a platform upon which to rest the binocular.) If there is nothing for him to prop his back against, and he has nothing else to support the binocular with, a hunter can try rolling as tightly forward in a sitting position as he can, with his elbows locked against his quads. The critical consideration when it comes to holding a binocular is that the less light there is, the more stable the binocular has to be, and the most reliable way to reduce the amplitude of movement is to bring down the viewing height as much as possible (*stay low to stay steady*).

* **Keeping It Working:** A hunter wants to avoid becoming fixated on a single image when using a binocular for extended periods in the field. Sheep hunters in particular—though the case is not far different for many other types of hunters—may spend hours glassing some cross-valley slope

in the hope of detecting a trace of a curled horn; in doing so there is a definite risk of suffering the binocular user's version of the truck driver's "white-line fever." A hunter can believe that if he doesn't keep staring directly at one spot, he will miss whatever is going to appear there. This thought process hews, of course, rather uncomfortably close to the clinical symptoms of insanity; but however it may be diagnosed, it inevitably results in a hunter's sinking into a sort of state of boredom-related catatonia in which his eyes simply stop moving and accommodating, and he ends up not seeing anything anyhow.

Spotting game is a matter of noting a change in the portrait of the landscape, however subtle. "There is one of the hunter's senses which must work indefatigably at all times. That is the sense of sight. Look, look, and look again. . ." Those are the words Edward, Count Yebes, author of *Veinte Años de Caza Mayor* ("Twenty Years of Big Game Hunting"), a book now utterly eclipsed by its prologue, written by the Spanish philosopher José Ortega y Gasset and published separately under the title *Un Tratadi de Montería* ("Meditations on Hunting"). Whatever Count Yebes' merits as a writer, his knowledge of hunting certainly went far deeper than his friend Ortega's; and his words are well worth heeding. But to "look, look, and look again" requires "fresh eyes," or eyes that are constantly being refreshed. This means that a hunter should not view in an uninterrupted panning movement but rather in a sequence of discrete frames, the way a motion picture is photographed.

When viewing a wide area, a hunter can, in his mind, break it up into a grid. Each square of the grid will be the area covered by the center of the binocular's field of view. A hunter can view each square carefully for a few seconds before moving on. The grid should not, though, be thought of as a pure two-dimensional plane. One of the most valuable features of the binocular, as has been noted, is its three-dimensional image-making; so if a hunter does not avail himself of that, he will not be using a binocular to its full potential. The "grid," therefore, should be thought of as rather more of a large transparent box or cube constructed out of small cubes, with the hunter viewing the small cubes from front to back, as well as side to side, within the depth of field of his binocular, adjusting his focus as needed. Making his way through this box will be a continuous, repeated process for a hunter, until something that had not been there for him before (as a guide once put it, "the strange, the unusual, the indifferent") is there now, demanding closer inspection. In practice, this technique takes a lot less thought than the explanation of it, and it quickly becomes an efficient and natural routine once a hunter trains himself to follow it.

CARRYING:

The entire raison d'être for the binocular, at least around a hunter's neck, is to show him things that he could not get a good look at without walking up on, something most wild game animals are unlikely to tolerate. And getting those good looks are not possible unless that binocular is, indeed, around a hunter's neck or on his person somewhere that is handy for him to get at to bring the binocular up to his eyes when he is in the field.

There are several ways of carrying a binocular:

- **The Neck Strap:** Nothing is more fundamental, of course, for carrying a binocular than a neck strap. Every new binocular comes with one, but such straps are often a narrow ribbon of woven nylon that by the end of a day in the field will likely feel to the back of a hunter's neck the way that wire cable on a cheese cutter feels to a wheel of Gouda. Better binoculars will come with wider, often padded, and consequently more comfortable straps, and there are also "after-market" straps made of neoprene or the like that can be found in camera stores or gunshops or in a catalog of hunting or optical products.

Whatever style of strap is chosen, it won't be worth a lick unless the binocular is securely attached to it. If the strap is threaded through the rings on the side of the binocular housing and then fed back up through one of those little buckles on the strap, there is always a risk of the strap slipping out of that buckle and the binocular falling from the hunter's neck. This kind of attachment can be secured by having a long enough tag end to the strap after it has been passed through the buckle and then taking that tag end and wrapping it around the strap and tying it off with a couple of half-hitches. If the strap has clips or hooks that connect it to the rings, then these should be regularly inspected to make sure they are still holding and aren't bent or no longer locking. And the strap itself should be occasionally examined for wear, cuts, or fraying.

The length of the strap is always somewhat problematic. If the binocular is worn on a long strap, it will swing out and back against a hunter's chest when he is walking, especially on slopes. One solution is for a hunter to shorten the strap so that the binocular rests high on his chest; when he lifts it to his eyes, the oculars will just clear his chin and nose. This will turn the binocular into much less of a pendulum. Alternatively, a hunter can lengthen the strap far enough to allow him to slip an arm through and have the strap running diagonally across his chest, then tuck the binocular around behind where it will ride on the small of his back without bumping against him and can still be swung back quickly for fast viewing.

- **The Harness:** Binocular harnesses, or suspenders, are marketed by several makers, but the design is essentially the same. It consists of two loops of elastic straps or surgical tubing that are joined in the back and fit around the shoulders. There are attachments on the fronts of each of the straps for the rings on the binocular. With the binocular in place, the two straps are held together and the binocular will be held firmly against the chest. Either the attachments on the straps slide up and down, or the straps themselves are stretchy enough to allow the binocular to be brought up easily for viewing through. An advantage of the harness is that it can greatly relieve strain on the neck by distributing the weight of the binocular through the chest, shoulders, and back.

- **The Pouch:** Rigs similar to the ones just described can also be used while wearing a carrying pouch on the chest. Pouches offer added impact protection for the binocular and can shield it from rain and snow. They can also come in a belt style that can be worn around the waist. A neck strap can be something of an inconvenience with a pouch, occupying too much room inside or getting tangled when the binocular is removed, and points to the major disadvantage of a pouch: There's a greater chance of a hunter's having the binocular slip from his hand and having no strap to save it or the far more likely scenario of the hunter's putting the binocular down for just a second on a rock or stump and forgetting it ever existed until he's 300 miles away. If it seems implausible that a hunter could forget about a fine piece of optics, consider that some years ago on a mule-deer hunt in

Alberta, the president of a well-known optics company began turning the camp upside down, searching for the high-end spotting scope he had brought with him. Matters turned slightly ugly when it became obvious that the president had begun to suspect that one of the other hunters or guides had availed himself of a "five-finger discount" on this scope. A frosty day or two later the president, another hunter, and a guide hiked back out to the river bluff from which the president had been glassing with the spotting scope on the first day of the hunt. Here is where the spotting scope was found, standing out in the wide open on its tripod, just the way the optics company president had left it when he'd gotten up and walked away from it almost a week earlier. And on that same hunt, another hunter awoke one morning and began looking for his bright, shiny Mark V 7-millimeter Weatherby Magnum rifle and could not find it. It took him several frantic minutes to realize he'd left it leaning against a fencepost the evening before while he waited to be picked up and driven back to the camp, and it took an even longer agonized period of time to drive back out and discover that this rifle, too, was still where the hunter had forgotten it. This was either dumb luck or a tribute to the fundamental integrity of our Canadian neighbors.

- **The Pocket:** Being able to fit into a pocket is why they are called "pocket binoculars." The drawbacks of even the best-quality pocket binocular, such as, say, a 6x20- or 8x20-millimeter, are all those matters of exit pupil, twilight factor, and relative brightness. There is simply no way around its lacking in these, which is why such a binocular shouldn't be a hunter's only, or even his primary, binocular. While a hunter should have at least one good 8x40- or 10x40-millimeter binocular as his optics of choice, the addition of a pocket model will not put him at a disadvantage. There are times, places, and conditions when, where, and under which a pocket binocular can be particularly handy (remember that Derringer that Paladin always carried along with his six-gun in *Have Gun, Will Travel*).

Africa comes to mind as a place where a pocket binocular could be of great use. Because much of the hunting in Africa takes place not far from the equator, the entire notion of "twilight" becomes somewhat less critical than it would be in the upper reaches of the Northern Hemisphere. In Africa the transition from day to dark and dark to day is extremely rapid, so a superb twilight factor is of somewhat lesser value. Light conditions will usually be such that a pocket binocular can provide a perfectly adequate view. On a long track for hours through the heat of midday, most hunters would prefer to have their binoculars residing comfortably in their shirt pockets rather than slung around their sweaty necks like the Ancient Mariner's albatross. And exactly how much exit pupil is required for spotting a Cape buffalo or an elephant? None of which is to say that a hunter packing for a safari should drop only his pocket binocular into his kit bag; there will definitely be occasions when he will want that 8x40-millimeter to part the leaves and branches of some thicket into which a bushbuck has ducked or to catch the last glint of light off a kudu horn, even if there isn't enough time left to make a stalk.

- **The Truck Dashboard:** Unfortunately, all too often the truck dashboard is where a binocular gets chucked when a hunter is moving to and from his hunting area, and it's a sorry place to carry any piece of optics for which a hunter has any regard. The dashboard may seem the most convenient location for the binocular, on the chance that the hunter will need it in a hurry to get a glimpse of something up ahead stepping into the trees, but on a strap or otherwise on his person is far better. On the dashboard the binocular will be, at best, rattled around and almost certainly tossed onto the floorboards after some particularly sharp jolt and will probably fall out onto the ground when the truck door is opened. A binocular is a *precision instrument* containing an assembly of sometimes dozens of *glass* elements. It is—at least a quality one is—built to be used in the cold, heat, rain, and snow and to withstand a reasonable amount of wear and tear. It is not, though, built to be abused, and it is possible for anyone to batter a binocular to pieces if he tries hard enough or, conversely, doesn't try at all—to treat it with respect, that is.

- **Miscellany:** As far as its qualities go, as was discussed earlier, a good hunting binocular needs to be fully waterproof and fogproof. These two qualities, though, refer to its internal workings. Mist and moisture can certainly cover the exterior of the objective and the eyepiece and interfere with viewing. Lens covers offer some protection. New binoculars will come with joined or elongated covers for the oculars that can be attached to the neck strap by the slots on the cover's ends and slid down over both eyepieces, shielding against precipitation. As a tip, it's generally better to run the strap through only one of the slots; when a hunter pulls off a cover attached in this fashion, he can push it to one side so it won't be in the way while he's viewing; as a further consideration, the slot that the strap is run through should be on the side opposite the shoulder on which a hunter mounts his firearm, keeping it farther out of the way if he has to drop his binocular and bring up his rifle.

Harnesses and pouches may not have straps to which to attach the cover, but a thin length of strong cord or the like can be threaded through one of the cover's slots, then through one of the rings on the binocular's body, and tied in a loop so the cover can be removed from the eyepieces and not fall off and be lost on the ground somewhere. As for the caps for the objectives, unless they are attached to the binocular body by straps or hinges or some like system, they should be left in the case when the binocular is removed because if they are merely stuck onto the objectives and taken out into the field, they are not coming back.

Another of the small touches that hunters should be on the lookout for is the size of the tabs on the covers for the objectives. When a hunter hurriedly raises his binocular, the objective covers almost always have to be flipped down, having somehow found their way back over the lenses, whether the hunter wanted them there or not. Too many of these covers have slim, low-profile tabs that can take several seconds to locate by feel and lack a generous surface to push against. The only way to say it is that a hunter should look for fat tabs on the objective-lens covers on any binocular he may need for a snap view in the field.

One more possibility for combating blurring moisture is the use of water-shedding coatings that some manufacturers are now applying to the exteriors of the objectives and eyepieces of their binoculars and other optics.

As far as cleaning lenses in the field, the injunction of the Roman physician Galen, *"Primum non nocere"*—"First, do no harm"—should be scrupulously adhered to. Keeping dust off the lenses—and this, to be sure, applies to all optics—is basic, but care must be taken that the process of dust removal does not turn into one of grinding the dust particles into the coated surface. If a hunter cannot puff away all the dust while he is in the field, he might want to settle for the slightly sparkly vantage and wait until he returns to camp or wherever he can do a proper job of cleaning. Not letting dust accumulate to begin with, by the use of lens covers, is a better approach, as is avoiding smearing the lenses with oily and acidic fingerprints. If a hunter is absolutely convinced that he will need to really clean his lenses in the field, then he might want to consider bringing along a lens pen, a small bottle of cleaning fluid, and a lens cloth or a package of lens tissues that can be found at an optician's or camera store, as can those individual packets of premoistened cleaning towelettes mentioned earlier. Again, though, dust will be the major culprit, so the most important consideration is removing it as gently as possible. This also means not transferring grit from the cleaning materials to the lens, which is why any of those materials that are brought into the field should be contained in something like a plastic zipper-lock bag so that they, too, will be as dust-free as possible.

SIDELIGHT:

"For want of a nail, the shoe was lost," wrote Benjamin Franklin; and it may have been for want of modern optics that Lieutenant-Colonel George Armstrong Custer rashly led more than two hundred men and officers of the Seventh Cavalry, along with five civilians—208 souls in all—into battle against as many as 2,500 Blackfeet, Northern Cheyenne, Sans Arcs, Oglala, Minneconjou, and Hunkpapa Lakota warriors and into history.

In early 1876 Lakota and other Indians began leaving their reservations and banding together. By late June of that year Custer and his cavalry were riding hard in blistering weather, southwest from the Yellowstone River, in search of a reported massive encampment of "renegade" Indians. Tribes were, indeed, collecting on the west bank of the Little Bighorn River, known to the Indians as the "Greasy Grass" for the nutritious feed found around it. The village that arose was not merely big but perhaps the largest ever to form on the Great Plains, with as many as fifteen thousand inhabitants.

In normal times no assemblage of these nomadic hunter-gatherer peoples would have ever grown so outsized because of such practical considerations as having sufficient buffalo to hunt, pasturage for the horses, wood to burn, even adequate sites for latrines. These were not normal times, though, and it may be that the Indians sensed an end to their old ways and a last chance to live the life they had always known. It could have been an opportunity no one wanted to let go by.

Custer's objective was to force these Indians back onto the reservations, and without knowing the true size of the village he was advancing on or exactly where it was to be found, he was nonetheless confident that his regiment of some six hundred military men, along with around fifteen armed civilians and thirty-five to forty Indian scouts, could accomplish that mission. On the night of June 24 Custer's Crow scouts (ancestral enemies of the Lakota, whom they considered invaders) reported to him that they believed the hostiles' encampment lay 25 miles to the west in the valley of the Little Bighorn. Custer ordered First Lieutenant Charles A. Varnum to go out from the bivouac at 9 p.m. with Crow and Arikara Indian scouts and the white scout Charlie Reynolds, to head for the divide between the Rosebud and Little Bighorn Rivers to a place that would famously become known as the "Crow's Nest," and to be there by dawn to observe the village and judge its size. Custer said he would follow at 11 p.m.

Varnum and his scouts were at the Crow's Nest before first light, and at dawn the Crow, with their naked eyes, saw the thousands of ponies and smoke of the innumerable campfires in the valley 15 miles away. Varnum immediately sent word back to Custer, who had halted after four hours of marching the night before. Custer finally reached the Crow's Nest in the late morning, but through his low-powered, undoubtedly high-dispersion-lens field glasses—and through the haze that had come up with the heat of the day—he was unable to see the "big village—many ponies—many Lakota" that the Crow scouts, such as White Man Runs Him, Goes Ahead, and Curley, were still able to make out.

Custer's scout Mitch Bouyer, whose father was a French fur trader and whose mother was a Santee Sioux and who had been born in what in 1868 became Wyoming Territory, knew the country here better than anyone. He reportedly told Custer, "Look for worms—the pony herd looks like worms moving on the grass."

Custer's field glasses still revealed nothing, and he declared, "My eyes are as good as yours, and I don't see any Indians." Bouyer continued to insist that they were facing insurmountable odds. A withering glance from Custer finally made Bouyer give in and agree to follow him.

The Crow were far less game. When it became clear to them that Custer was not going to believe the evidence of their own eyes, they began removing their Army-issued black felt hats with red-and-white cords around the crowns, Civil War surplus blue cavalry shell jackets, and red bandanas that identified them as scouts and donning their tribal battle dress. When asked by Custer what they were doing, they replied that they preferred to die as Crow warriors rather than as U.S. soldiers. In one interpretation of the event, Custer told them they had fulfilled their obligation to lead him to the village and, disgusted by their apparent fatalism, relieved them of any further duty, letting them ride off. In another interpretation, he dismissed them without prejudice, in fact taking it as an encouraging sign that they were not eager to engage in face-to-face combat, assuming that the Indians in the village would not be, either. The other scouts, the

Arikara and in particular Bloody Knife, felt a loyalty to Custer that compelled them to go on with him, though not before painting themselves and singing their death songs.

After that, Custer led his regiment forward, dividing it into three battalions—in fact, four, counting the pack train as a separate contingent—and with his own five companies forded the river at Medicine Tail Coulee at a charge and fell headlong into a hill of stinging ants. According to Northern Cheyenne warrior Two Moons, the time it took for Custer to destroy the men under his command and to lose his own life on the battlefield was no more than what it takes "a hungry man to eat his dinner." (In all, counting the losses suffered by Custer's two other commanders, Major Marcus Reno and Captain Frederick Benteen, in holding out on high ground after the "Last Stand" and those of the Indian warriors, 406 lives were taken in the two days of fighting.)

The story of Custer's field glasses does not end there. To the victors went the spoils; and after the battle the Lakota and their allies, especially the women, salvaged everything of value from the field, down to the cavalrymen's clothes and boots. There is a photo, for example, posed for in a studio sometime after the battle, of Touch the Clouds, the seven-foot-tall cousin of Crazy Horse and chief of the Minneconjou, holding a rifle that appears to be Custer's own Remington No. 1 .50-70 sporting rifle that is known to have been with him on June 25.

Custer also had his field glasses. These were apparently kept by a Minneconjou or Hunkpapa for another fourteen years. In 1890 the Lakota were caught up in the "Ghost Dance" movement, spread by a Paiute prophet known as "Wovoka" who preached that if all tribes performed the Ghost Dance, then the buffalo would return, and the dead would be brought back to life. As the Ghost Dance spread, the whites in charge of the reservations began to fear that this signaled the start of new warfare by the Indians.

At the end of that year fate seemed to take a tragic hand in the affairs of the Lakota and the whites who considered the Lakota their charges. In mid-December Sitting Bull, the Indian commander at Greasy Grass, was killed by tribal police when they tried to arrest him on government orders on the Standing Rock Reservation in South Dakota. Members of Sitting Bull's tribe fled Standing Rock and joined with Big Foot, father of Touch the Clouds, on the Cheyenne River and then, with Big Foot and his people, started for Pine Ridge and the sanctuary that they believed Red Cloud, the great Oglala chief, could provide.

Five hundred men of the same Seventh Cavalry that had endured Custer's defeat intercepted Big Foot's band and marched it to Wounded Knee Creek. Here the Army placed four Hotchkiss light mountain guns around the Indians' camp. This was the season known to the Lakota as the "moon of the popping trees," and during the bitterly cold night of December 28 the rumor spread among the Indians that they were to be deported to Oklahoma. The military's interpreter was not fluent in the dialect that Big Foot and his people spoke and in translating their speeches managed to make them sound bellicose to the white troops, who were also drinking in celebration of the capture.

The next morning the cavalry ordered the Lakota to disarm in order to maintain peace. A medicine man began a Ghost Dance and called on others to join. He told them that the ceremonial "Ghost Shirts" they wore would turn away any Army bullets. Then a trooper tried to take a gun away from a deaf Lakota who struggled with him, believing he was being accused of theft. At that point a shot was fired somewhere, and the medicine man, Yellow Bird, is said to have thrown a handful of dust into the air, which was misinterpreted by the troopers as a signal for the Indians to attack.

The fighting along the creek was at close quarters at first; then the Lakota, mostly women and children, ran to their lodges, where some had hidden weapons. Buffalo hide, fortifications, and small arms proved no defense against artillery. In the time it takes to eat a leisurely supper at home, 153 Lakota and 25 men of the cavalry were dead. In a reversal of roles from that at Greasy Grass, it was the turn of the men of the Seventh Calvary to strip the corpses. On the body of one Lakota were field glasses (through which, perhaps, this Lakota had watched the last bison on the plains) recognized as those that had belonged to George Custer.

There is a bill of sale for these field glasses, written in 1897 by a trooper to his brother, stating:

> Nearly all of the officers of the 7th U.S. Cavalry have inspected these glasses and expressed themselves as being convinced that they were the actual glasses used by General Custer in the campaign in which he and his gallant troopers were massacred.

The quality of George Armstrong Custer's field glasses may have spelled his defeat.

This bill of sale established the provenance of these field glasses when they were auctioned in 2005. The winning bid was $56,625, working out, between Greasy Grass and Wounded Knee, including Indians and whites, to something less than $100 per life.

THE RIFLESCOPE   **5**

It is the accepted wisdom that credit for the invention of the riflescope should go to yet another Teuton. This was the Austrian August Fiedler, who served as a forestry commissioner to Bohemian Prince Reuss IV. Fiedler is said to have built the first adjustable riflescope in 1880. Eighteen years later Karl Robert Kahles (not to be confused with Kahless the Unforgettable, legendary patriarch of the Klingon Empire) produced in his Vienna Optical Manufactury a commercial version of the adjustable riflescope, which would be marketed under the name of "Telorar." On the basis of this, the Kahles company stakes its claim to being the world's oldest maker of riflescopes. Nonetheless, adjustable riflescopes were being built and sold in the United States a half-century earlier. And not even those were the ur-source of the riflescope. To discover where that may lie, it is necessary to return to the advent of the rifled barrel and before. It would even probably be best to begin with gunpowder.

Sometime during the eleventh century AD, Chinese alchemists were believed to have discovered the explosive properties of potassium nitrate. KNO_3—known as "saltpeter," *sal
petrae*," "stone salt," and what the Arabs of the time called "Chinese snow," enshrined in urban legend as an antiaphrodisiac
sprinkled liberally by the U.S. military onto the food of its own
troops, who claimed they could detect it by the green tinge it lent
the eggs in their morning chow—was combined by alchemists
with other ingredients to produce a kind of proto-gunpowder to
make rockets and firecrackers. Later, primarily for shock-and-
awe value on the battlefield, the Chinese developed "fire lances"
to launch incendiary gunpowder bombs and bamboo tubes to fire
clay pellets.

It is further believed that the Arabs obtained the knowledge
of gunpowder from the Chinese and brought it to Spain, which
they then dominated; and it was from Spain that the polymath
Roger Bacon received the formula for what would become in
1248 the first published prescription for the making of real gunpowder from saltpeter, sulfur, and charcoal, concealed as an ana-
gram within his *Epistolae de secretis operibus artis et naturae, et
de nullitate magiae* ("The Letter Concerning the Marvelous
Power of Art and Nature and the Nullity of Magic.")

With a recipe for gunpowder, there appeared the *hand-
gonne,* the English word of the day for firearms that could be carried as opposed to emplaced guns such as cannons. As early as
1281 Count Guido da Montefeltro—later condemned by Dante
Alighieri to the torments of his *Inferno* for the sin of false coun-
sel—was reportedly at the head of a squad of "crossbowmen and
scopetteri" (troops carrying portable guns) marching into battle
under the flag of the Emilia-Romagna city of Forlì.

The word *gun* is derived from a woman's name, *Gunilda,*
which was given to a *ballista,* a giant crossbow used as a siege engine to launch heavy projectiles to breach fortifications, carried on

the munitions list of Windsor Castle in 1330. The name "Gunilda" itself is a compound of two Old Norse words, both meaning "war": *gunnr* and *hildr*. The first handheld guns were smoothbores and lacked any aiming device other than the gunner's raising the end of the barrel into alignment with the top of the *serpentine lock*— the *S*-shaped piece of metal that held at one end a smoldering match-cord and that was levered up at the other end to lower the match-cord into contact with the gun's touchhole and ignite the powder charge in the gun.

The *rifled barrel* (a gun barrel the length of whose inner diameter, or *bore,* is cut with helical "lands" and "grooves" known as *rifling* that impart rotation to the projectile when it is fired) has been around since perhaps the late 1400s, along with recognizable front and rear sights. The vast improvements that these made in the gun—now with these additions renamed the *rifle*— were indisputable, especially from the standpoint of hunters. The only stumbling block to wide acceptance of the rifle was the struggle to ram a ball down the barrel so that it engaged the rifling. Primarily for that reason, smoothbore muskets remained the preferred military small arm for several centuries; and so gunmakers, for whom armies were their biggest customers, did not much trifle with producing rifles.

In the eighteenth century the English scientist, mathematician, and engineer Benjamin Robins—curiously the son of Quakers—conducted extensive experimental studies of all aspects of gunnery, including the advantages of the rifled barrel. At this time, and for nearly ninety years after Robins's death, the mainstay of the British Army was the "Land Pattern Musket," the .75-caliber "Brown Bess." The guns were relatively short-range weapons in terms of accuracy, no more than 100 yards. They were meant to be fired in mass formations: During an attack a battalion assembled itself into a 300-yard-wide line ranked two deep, while for defense it would assemble itself into a four-deep square. The concept was not so much one of waiting-for-the-whites-of-the-enemies'-eyes and squeezing off a well-aimed shot as it was listening for the command "Fire!" and hoping the opposing force would be mowed down by a proverbial hail of gunfire. If the enemy advanced through the fusillades, then it was time for "Tommy Atkins" to bring his musket's spike bayonet into play.

The influence of Robins's work upon the British Army, though, began to be seen during the Napoleonic Wars with the introduction of the .625-caliber Baker rifle and the formation in 1800 of the Ninety-Fifth Regiment of the Foot, an "Experimental Corps of Riflemen" known as the "Green Jackets" for their distinctive uniforms. The members of this regiment were raised by Colonel Coote Manningham and Lieutenant-Colonel the Honorable William Stewart from the ranks of enlisted men and officers and became the British Army's first sharpshooters and scouts. Naturally, being British, they were some twenty-five years late.

In 1775 Captain Daniel Morgan of the American Continental Army recruited "Morgan's Sharpshooters," these marksmen's Long Rifles so disconcerting to the British during the Revolutionary War that officers removed any visible insignia from their uniforms in order to make themselves less conspicuous targets. In 1847 a French Army captain, Claude Etienne Minié, invented a conical bullet with a hollow bottom (a "Minié ball") that embodied Robins's ballistic theories. Easy to load in a rifled firearm, the Minié expanded at the rear from the gas pressure of the burning gunpowder and gripped the rifling with its sides, or "bearing surfaces." Accurate rifle fire was now not only available but also widely practicable, elevating the demand for more precise aiming devices.

Again, front-and-rear iron sights on a rifle were nothing new, even in the nineteenth century. By the end of that century, though, three basic styles of those sights had evolved:

- An aperture or **peep** sight has a small perforated disk or a circle (sometimes called a *ghost ring* for the way in which it blurs in the hunter's vision as he aims through it and focuses on the front sight) mounted on the rear of the action or on the tang on the top of the grip, and a bead, post, or even another aperture at the front of the barrel (often referred to as a *globe* sight, this is a cylinder or "hood" that acts as a sunshade and inside of which may be inserted different "aiming reference marks," such as posts or crosshairs). To take aim, the shooter centers the top of the notch or the whole bead, or the center of the other aperture and mark, in the rear circle.

- A **notch-and-post** sight is one in which the rear "notch" portion is usually mounted on the barrel just ahead of the action, depending on the type of action and firearm, and could be a *U, V,* or square shape (called a "Partridge" after its inventor E. E. Partridge, one of the founders in 1875 of the Massachusetts Rifle Association, and a sight still in extensive use on many present-day handguns) and has a front post, blade, or bead that is set in the middle of the notch, level with its top.

- The **buckhorn** sight resembles its name with the rear portion in the shape of the horns of a pronghorn with the tips turning in (or with two less severe wings) to create an aiming window, with a small notch at the bottom for the bead or the top of the post to nest in.

A near hybrid of the buckhorn and the notch-and-post sights is the *express* sight, which utilizes a wide shallow *V* and a front bead that is usually white (ivory was often used for the bead, warthog ivory being preferred because it was less likely to yellow with age). The sight is named for its function, which is to be used quickly, often on dangerous game at close quarters, and so it is most frequently seen on heavy caliber bolt-action or double "stopping" rifles. It, as well as any other notch-and-post sight, may also have several folding rear sights that can be flipped up for varying yardages. The express sight, too, has been around since at least the nineteenth century, as has the front-bead or the ribbed-bead sight on a shotgun, in which the rear sight is the hunter's eye— making it essential that the shotgun shooter mount the gun firmly to his cheek every time to bring his eye into the proper line with the front bead. About the only twentieth-century advancement on the iron sight has been the addition of fiber-optic materials that create the impression of glowing beads in the sight.

The distance between the front and rear sight on the firearm is known as the *sight radius;* for sights of equal quality, the longer the radius, the more accurately the firearm may be aimed. The correct alignment of the sights, front and rear, has been described earlier, but the aligned sights must still be brought into a proper relationship with the target. This is known as the *sight picture. Hold* may be the most important factor in the sight picture, and this is a matter of some contention. The big-end-of-the-egg versus the small-end-of-the-egg argument boils down to holding the sight either "dead center" or "six o'clock." With a dead-center hold on, say, the back of a penny, the shooter would have a sight picture placing the top of the aligned sights squarely in the middle of the Lincoln Monument. For a six-o'clock hold, the bottom rim of the penny would be balanced on the top of the sights like a ball on a seal's nose. These holds are a matter of the shooter's preference, though the six-o'clock hold has a far greater following perhaps because it obscures less of the target; in either case, at the moment the shot is fired, the only object in sharp focus should be the front sight.

Unless a firearm has fixed sights—and those are likely to be found only on handguns of usually older design such as the Colt Peacemaker—iron sights may be adjusted to accommodate either type of hold—in fact the sights on a Peacemaker or the like may be adjusted, too, by filing down the front blade sight although this will only succeed in raising the point of impact. Rear aperture sights may have extremely fine, nearly micrometric adjustment capabilities for both *elevation* (up *or* down) and *windage* (right and left), while a notch-and-post or buckhorn sight can have screws to loosen the rear sight to allow for it to be moved up and down on a ramp and for the ramp to be moved right and left. Or these sights may ride on a small spring-tensioned tang attached to the barrel and have a sawtoothed stepped elevator that can slide forward or back when the sight is lifted. To adjust the windage on such sights, it is usually necessary to *drift* them one way or another by gently tapping on the dovetail tenon holding the sight on the barrel.

The Unalterable Law of Adjustment:
With iron sights a hunter moves the rear sight in the direction he wants the point of impact to move; if he is adjusting the front sight, he moves it in the *opposite* direction—up for down, right for left, etc.

Iron sights can be capable of extremely precise adjustment and pinpoint accuracy. Peep sights are superb but save their best work for the target range, presenting the hunter with a constricted sight picture. For field use ghost rings work well, and buckhorns may be the iron sight of choice for all-around field use, but they are likely to be able to be only coarsely adjusted. And as hunters age, and their eyes with them *(presbyopia)*, the issue of sight radius can become critical (legend has it that the barrel of a mountain man's Hawken rifle might exhibit a series of dovetail mortises indicating that the rear sights were moved progressively farther down the barrel as the hunter-trapper got older and his eyes literally less accommodating). Whether by predilection or inevitability, rifle hunters will find themselves using a riflescope, sooner or later. They can, though, take comfort in the fact that they are in no way profaners by peering through one. The telescopic sight on a rifle, and even a handgun, is a centuries-old tradition, dating back to a time before bicycles first had pedals.

Bicycle pedals appeared in 1839, and the first reportedly verifiable instance of a firearm with a telescopic sight was a handgun in 1834. There are accounts, though, of optical sights being used on firearms that date back to the time of the telescope's invention and a story that even Newton tried putting one of his catoptric telescopes on a gun.

By the end of the eighteenth century, American gunsmiths were building long, full-stocked target rifles with double set triggers. These rifles also had "tube sights," which consisted of a crosshair mounted inside a lenseless tube to prevent glare on the crosshairs so that they remained clear to the shooter. Even greater accuracy became possible in the 1820s with the invention of the percussion cap—frequently and incorrectly credited to the Scottish Reverend Alexander Forsythe, who did invent a percussion *lock;* the most likely innovator of the percussion *cap* was Joseph Egg of Picadilly, London, son of the renowned Swiss gunmaker Durs Egg, and proprietor of "Joseph Egg & Sons, Gun, Rifle & Pistol Manufacturers To the Royal Family" and "Inventors of the Copper Cap and Patentees of Self Priming Percussion Guns." Rifles could now arguably shoot beyond the capabilities of their aiming systems.

The invention of the optical riflescope is thought to have taken place in the United States sometime between 1835 and 1840. In 1844 a British civil engineer, John Ratcliffe Chapman, wrote *Instructions to Young Marksmen, in All that Relates to the General Construction, Practical Manipulation, Causes and*

Liability to Error in Making Accurate Rifle Performances, and the Theoretic Principles upon Which Such Accurate Performances Are Founded, as Exhibited in the Improved American Rifle. In that book, not much longer than its title, he disparages the "shorter" riflescopes that had "been in use for some time" and states that "so far as sighting is concerned, [the] telescope [sight], properly made and properly fixed, is nearer perfection than any other method of sighting known." Chapman's description of a riflescope "which will perform perfect at all times" is of a "3 feet 1 inch long" tube fashioned from either "good and stiff" sheet iron or the preferred sheet steel, "5/8ths of an inch diameter outside, and 1/20th of an inch thick, weighing about 10 ounces."

Chapman had "once thought of securing by patent" the riflescope he so lavishly praised but "found that the trouble and expense would overbalance the profit." He does provide the reader, though, with the information that the Utica, New York, rifle maker Morgan James had invented his own plan for mounting the crosshairs so that they "cannot be affected by the vibration of the weapon, and particular attention is paid to the *seating of the lenses* [italics Chapman's], and the fastening and fitting of the tubes in which they are set, to the tube of the telescope." These scopes included erecting systems, and they were sold, with mounts, by James for $20, or about $520 today.[vi] Chapman also does not say that most optics of the time were usually not more than 3X or 4X; and it would be reasonable to assume that with a 5/8th-inch-diameter tube made from 1/20th-inch-thick steel the objective would be something like 10.8 millimeters, which would work out to a relatively decent exit pupil of 3.6 at 3X and a 9.9 twilight factor. Chapman also fails to mention that he and James would soon be going into partnership to manufacture these riflescopes, thus nurturing, if not originating, the grand tradition of hunting-optics writers' flacking for products in which they have a veiled financial interest.

A Leatherwood/
HiLux replica
Malcolm scope on
a custom black-
powder rifle.
Photo © 2007 Toby
Bridges. Used with
permission.

In 1855 in Syracuse, New York, William Malcolm became the first mass producer of riflescopes. Malcolm did not borrow from Chapman and James but rather worked for a telescope maker to learn his craft and design his own scope. His included achromatic lenses and highly refined external adjustments, and his riflescopes could achieve magnifications of 20X and higher.

Malcolm's scopes, and those of another maker, L. M. Amidon of Vermont, became standard among Union sharpshooters during the Civil War. In the summer of 1861 Hiram Berdan began recruiting eighteen companies of these marksmen. Berdan, a mechanical engineer in New York City, had been made wealthy by his inventions, such as a repeating rifle and an amalgamation machine for separating gold from ore. For fifteen years prior to the war, he was the top sporting rifle shot in the country. To join his sharpshooters, a soldier had to place ten consecutive shots into a 10-inch bull at 200 yards.

The sharpshooters were originally issued five-shot revolving Colt rifles but soon switched to the .50-70 Berdan Sharps, while many carried their own personal 30-pound target rifles with scopes. The sharpshooters became a particularly effective psywar element in Union battle plans, adept at striking down Confederate artillerymen who thought they were safely beyond the reach of all rifle fire. The sharpshooters were also of tactical value in many engagements, particularly at Gettysburg. There the withering fire of 100 sharpshooters during the second day of the battle led Brigadier General Cadmus Marcellus Wilcox of the First Corps of the Army of Northern Virginia to conclude that he was facing at least two Union regiments. Meanwhile, as a brevet major general, Berdan gained the reputation of being "thoroughly unscrupulous and unreliable" and "totally unfit for a command." He resigned his commission in early 1864 and went on to invent a distance fuse for shrapnel, a submarine gunboat, and a long-distance rangefinder.

While the record of the riflescope's use in the Civil War is well-documented, its later employment in hunting, especially on the Great Plains by the buffalo hunters, is less so. Perhaps those long-tubed scopes did not stand up acceptably to the harsh handling they had to endure when hundreds of rounds might be fired through a rifle in a single day, day in and day out. Or maybe there was no special call for a scope for "hunting" a gigantic ungulate who, at least in the first years of the slaughter, would hold its ground while a shooter crawled into position and then would remain there as it bled out from a bullet wound while the rest of its bellowing herd clustered around it to share its fate. Whatever the cause, it seems that it was not until the 1920s and '30s that the riflescope began to draw the attention of American hunters.

One of the most famous names in riflescopes was also one of the most famous in rifles: Winchester. In 1907 Professor Charles Sheldon Hastings of Yale University (who during World War I helped design an extremely accurate sniper's rifle and scope) devised a rather curious process for building a target scope with intentional inaccuracies in the objective that would be corrected by the ocular in order to prevent competitors from duplicating the system. He sold T. G. Bennett, president of Winchester, on the oddball notion, and the company produced the A5 scope until it sold the manufacturing equipment and rights to the Lyman Gun Sight Corporation of Middlefield, Connecticut, in 1928.

The A5 was apparently not thought much of in its day, while Lyman's redesigned version, the 5A, was said to be a fine piece of optics. In the late 1930s Lyman would use Bausch & Lomb polarized lenses in the production of its 2½X (this was at a time when experts would pronounce a 5X riflescope to be "more or less useless as a hunting scope") "Alaskan" with 5-inch eye relief and one MOA *(see the "adjustment turret" following)* click internal adjustments, which remains something of a classic to this day.

In 1932 Kentucky hunter, shooter, and engineer William Ralph Weaver established the W. R. Weaver Company in El Paso, Texas, and began building what was considered the first practical, low-priced hunting riflescope, the 3-30. He soon followed this with the 2½ x 330 and the 4 x 440, though neither was considered stout enough to stand up to .30-'06 recoil. At the opposite end of the price spectrum were the scopes of the Unertl Optical Company, located at 75B Cemetery Lane in Pittsburgh, Pennsylvania, and founded in 1934 by John Unertl Sr., a German immigrant who had learned his optical trade during World War I in the German army's sight-manufacturing shop in Spandau.

Unertl's scopes were praised as the strongest and finest built in the United States at the time and more than the equal of any foreign import, and today its 10X Tactical scope, originally built for the United State Marine Corps, enjoys an enthusiastic cult following, in spite of a $2,500 price tag.

On the wagon journey west to the Oregon Territory, John Hill Redfield's mother had been wounded while she and her husband fought off an Indian attack. Within a few years, though, she was recovered enough to give birth to Redfield in Glendale, Oregon, in 1859. As a teenager, Redfield made his way to San Francisco, taking with him the hunting and shooting skills he'd learned around the family farm. As a gambler, meat hunter for the railroads, and deputy U.S. marshal, he found his way into Nevada and Idaho before returning to Oregon to open a gunsmith shop in Medford in 1893 and to marry the following year. Redfield was drawn to the mining boom in Colorado in 1906, bringing with him a rock drill of his own design. In 1909 in Denver he began the Redfield Gun Sight Company, which produced fine quality iron sights and scope mounts before producing hunting riflescopes themselves after World War II. At its peak in the mid-1960s Redfield's 125 employees were making 125,000 riflescopes per year. The original company remained in business for nearly ninety years, until millions of dollars in fines levied against it by the Environmental Protection Agency for groundwater contamination forced it out of business.

One more German immigrant of note in the history of American riflescopes was Markus Frederich "Fred" Leupold (pronounced *LOO-poled*). Born in Ravensburg, Germany, in 1875, he came to the United States in 1891, eventually finding work as a precision machinist with a Boston surveying-instrument manufacturer. Leupold later moved to Portland, Oregon, where his brother-in-law, Adam Voelpel, financed the survey-equipment-repair shop Leupold started in 1907.

In 1911 Leupold and Voelpel began manufacturing their own survey instruments but soon found it difficult to compete with larger, already-established companies. They then met John Cyprian Stevens, formerly a hydrologist for the U.S. Geological Survey who held a patent for an improved water-flow recorder. By the 1940s the company's recorders and surveying equipment were being sold all around the world. Volpel (he had changed the spelling of his name to avoid anti-German prejudice during World War I) died in 1942 and Fred Leupold in 1944. By then Leupold's sons Norbert and Marcus and Stevens's son Robert were running the company, and during World War II the company repaired merchant marine telescopic sights and learned that replacing the oxygen inside the sights with dry nitrogen eliminated internal fogging.

The Leupold company is also the source of one of the most enduring legends of American scope-making. While hunting blacktail deer in the perpetual rainstorms of Oregon's Cascade Range, Marcus Leupold missed a shot at a buck because he was unable to see it through the fogged scope on his rifle. Both angry and inspired, Leupold was determined to produce a more reliable riflescope based on the company's experience with the merchant marine sights. In 1947 the company introduced the Plainsman hunting riflescope and two years later incorporated under the name of Leupold & Stevens. The Plainsman was in keeping with the prevailing opinion of the day about power, being a fixed 2½X;

Diagram of a riflescope.

and while it did exhibit the innovation of nitrogen purging, all the windage and elevation adjustments were made in the mounts, as they had been in riflescopes for more than a century.

Even by the time of the Plainsman, the fundamental design of the modern riflescope had been fixed. The basic structure of then and today consists of the following components:

- The **main tube body** is formed by an extrusion of aircraft aluminum, titanium or steel, afterward undergoing a second extrusion process to create the *bell housings* that will hold the objective and the ocular lenses. Tube diameter can vary, but the two main choices are "1-inch" (25.4 millimeters) or "30 millimeter" (1.18 inches). Assuming that the manufacturer indeed uses larger-diameter erector lenses in the 30-millimeter tube, rather than simply using the same ones he puts into his 1-inch models and placing bigger mountings inside (the riflescope equivalent of "falsies"), that the 30-millimeter tube is not overly long, *and* that good-quality 30-millimeter rings and bases are available for it, it will have the advantage of less, or at least farther from the center, spherical aberration, more main-body stiffness, and a wider range of adjustments for elevation and windage, compared with a 1-inch scope of comparable quality, although in practice a hunter would be hard pressed to detect any difference in performance. The outer finish on the scope is a matter of both taste and serviceability. It can be anything from a glossy blue-black to matte black to matte chrome to camouflage and even anodized in assorted colors and abstract designs. Perhaps the only finish to be wary of, beyond the question of vulgarity, is that shiny one, likely to spook off the game if the light hits it just right.

It is hoped that the objective, ocular, and erector lenses have already been sufficiently illuminated in past chapters, along with such other considerations as waterproofing and fogproofing, coatings, exit pupil, etc.

• The **adjustment turret** (and it is assumed that most hunters today will be employing modern scopes with *internal* adjustments rather than the *external* ones found on vintage scopes like the Malcolm) sits very much in the heart of the main tube body and has *adjustment knobs* (they may be knobs, or they may be flat dials with single slots like the head of a screw) covered with caps. These knobs control the elevation and windage needed to zero the crosshairs on the target (i.e., bring the point of aim into coincidence with the point of impact). The adjustments on the knobs are usually broken down into fractions of *minutes of arc* or *minutes of angle* (both abbreviated as "MOA"). Either term refers to a 1/60th division of one degree of arc, known as a *minute*. As the total piece of a full circle, a minute would amount to roughly .0046 percent of it, or .0166 degree. If a hunter slightly modifies the mathematical formula for determining field of view at 1,000 yards *(described earlier)*, he will calculate that a single minute of arc subtends about 1 inch at 100 yards:

52.5 X .0166° X 1.2 = 1.05 inches @ 100 yards

The fractional divisions on the adjustment knobs for each "click" or each graduation on the dial can be from one-eighth to one MOA, but on most scopes it will be one-quarter. Anyone who has ever spent any amount of time at a shooting range has seen the geezer at the bench next to him fire his rifle on its rest, eject the empty cartridge, check his point of impact through his spotting scope, then make adjustments to the elevation and windage knobs on the turret of his scope. And without fail, the last thing he will do is pick up that empty brass and gently tap the knobs with the cartridge head. The explanation for this, other than being a psychology-textbook example of Skinnerian superstitious behavior, is that the erector tube holding the reticle inside the main body tube is held in position at one end by a pivoting mount known as a *gimbal* and at the other end against the adjustment pads by a *biasing spring*. This spring fatigues and becomes less responsive to adjustment with time and may not return fully to zero when recovering from the recoil of a shot. From past experience, or the wisdom of the ages, the old-timer taps the knobs to "set" the adjustments. (At least one riflescope company, Meade-Simmons, in the last few years has devised a new system for the erector tube that does away with the gimbal and spring, replacing them with special grooves and a new—unnamed—material that permits the tube to be adjusted while remaining firmly attached to the inside of the main tube body.)

- The **variable magnification band** (a '60s rock group?) and **power selector ring** (the object of a quest by elves and dwarves?) are two names for the knurled ring at the front of the ocular bell that is used to change the magnification on variable-power scopes. The whole discussion of magnification in riflescopes is a never-less-than-heated one. Seventy years ago the "2½-power" riflescope was "the recognized ideal . . . for miscellaneous American big-game hunting." Today no one would consider carrying anything less than a 4X, or more like a 6X, scope into the field; and most hunters will have a variable. The popularity of the variable riflescope, such as the ubiquitous 3–9X, has much to do with optics manufacturers having convinced hunters to buy what the optics manufacturers most want to sell them. As well, many hunters have a "more-is-more"—or "more-just-scratches-the-surface"—mentality toward scopes; and so it is possible to find big-game hunters in the field with rifles topped with Heffalump variables in the 4–16X or even 6–24X class, scopes far better suited to shooting varmints.

None of that is to diminish the worth of a variable rifle-scope under the right circumstances. A strong position can certainly be taken for a hunter's having a ruggedly built (to withstand magnum recoil) 1–4X scope on a dangerous-game rifle, that 1X offering the gigantic exit pupil and rapid target acquisition, without having to be befuddled by sight alignment. This type of scope is superior to even express sights at close quarters when the time comes to hit a charging something that has hooves, horns, tusks, claws, or teeth. And a 3–9X is a very sensible choice for conditions that can include dim light or long distances, as well as offering other benefits. (More about this in the section on the "reticle.")

Still, there is sort of mathematical elegance to a fixed-power riflescope that cannot be denied. And a scope might as well be an esthetic pleasure along with a working tool.

- Past the power ring comes a smaller **ocular** or **eyepiece focus locking ring**. (Some scopes do not have a locking ring.) In order to bring the reticle into precise focus for his aiming eye, a hunter, before he begins the sighting-in process with a scope, will place his scope-mounted *unloaded* rifle on a solid rest and aimed at a light background. He will then turn the bell until the image of the reticle goes just past the point of sharpest focus, then return the focus precisely to the sharpest point. If the reason for doing it this way is not, well, clear by now, it is simply because the human eye can't recognize the sharpest focus until it has actually seen it in the process of going beyond it. Trying to creep up on exact focus is like those ball carriers who showboat for the last 5 yards and get the football stripped from their hands by the defensive end—they never quite make it to the goal. When the reticle is focused, the locking ring can be tightened to hold it in position.

- The **parallax adjustment band**, if there is one, will usually be found on the objective bell, although sometimes it may be a third adjustment knob on the turret. Mark Twain would have described "parallax" as something that every hunter talks about but nobody knows anything about. It is in fact a fairly straightforward concept to bend the mind, or rather the scope image, around. The word derives from the Greek for "alteration" and is defined as an "apparent shift of an object against a background caused by a change in observer position." In a riflescope, parallax is caused by the inability of the scope to remain focused at all distances, particularly farther ones. Parallax can be seen in a riflescope by a hunter's holding the reticle on a target and then moving his eye around the ocular and noting whether or not the target moves in relation to the reticle. In the worst-case scenario, parallax can seriously affect the accuracy of the scope. Not all scopes, though, will come with parallax adjustments. Most scopes that might reasonably be used for big-game hunting will come from the factory already adjusted to be parallax-free at 100 yards (and sometimes at 50 yards for scopes intended for use on shotguns and muzzleloaders), and they shouldn't be substantially bothered by parallax for at least 200 yards beyond that. But for scopes higher than 10X and at extreme ranges, a parallax adjustment can be critical, and a band or knob will carry graduations for adjusting out to 400 or 500 yards or more and then to infinity (which may be represented by the graduation symbol oo).

- The word **reticle** comes down from the Latin word for "net" and is related to "reticule" which is a woman's knitted handbag; but "reticle" is just a highfalutin word for "crosshair." The reticle does lie at the hypocenter of hunting optics, though. The entire reason for being of all the other types of optical devices that a hunter uses in the field, even the riflescope itself, is to enable him to place the single-dimension aiming point of the reticle on the animal being pursued.

  The reticle is said to have been invented by one of van Leeuwenhoek's seventeenth-century contemporaries, the English biologist and eclectic and indefatigable experimenter, Robert Hooke. Renowned for his work in microscopy, Hooke was also a surveyor, and so it is most likely that it was in this equipment that the crosshair first appeared. The styles of reticles are numerous, from "fine" to "dot" to "duplex," and with thick-and-thin posts that can be further categorized from "fine" to "heavy duplex." A hunter's choice of reticle is dependent on the type of hunting he will be doing.

  A fine reticle or crosshair would be well suited to shooting prairie dogs at vast yardages on bright sunny High Plains days, the thin wires less likely to obscure the small rodents as they stand barking on the rims of their burrows. In dense hardwoods in the gloaming, the heavier posts of a duplex reticle would be more easily seen in reference to the animal (suggesting that a duplex of some kind might be an acceptable all-around choice). An extreme example is the "#4" duplex that has heavy posts on steroids and which was developed for the German *Weidmann* ("huntsman"or "hunter") to accommodate the conditions found in stalking wild boar in blanketed snow in the forest on moonlit nights without benefit of artificial lights.

The riflescope has two focal planes inside: one in front of the erector and the other behind; the reticle can be in either the *first focal plane* or the *second focal plane*. On a fixed-power scope this is of no importance. On a variable-power scope, though, a "first-focal-plane reticle" will increase or decrease in size as the power is changed (more magnification, bigger reticle, and vice versa), while a "second-focal-plane reticle" will remain the same size.

The "which-focal-plane?" question becomes important if a hunter is using a *mil-dot* riflescope. A *mil* is another unit of measure for a circle, like MOA. *Mil* is an abbreviation of *milliradian,* a *radian* being the angle that subtends an arc of a circle that is equal in length to the radius of that circle (e.g., a 10-inch-diameter circle would have a radius of 5 inches, and therefore the angle of a radian of that circle would subtend 5 inches of the circle's circumference). Put another way, a mil is approximately 1/6283rd of a circle, or about .057 degree. Effectively, the way this works out is that a mil subtends slightly less that 3.6 inches at 100 yards. In a first-focal-plane riflescope, the linear amount of this subtension will remain unchanged no matter what power of magnification the riflescope is set at. With second-focal-plane reticles, this 3.6-inch subtension will apply at a particular power setting, one that the manufacturer should indicate in the instruction manual.

To use mil dots to estimate ranges, the width or height of a known object will be measured in the number of dots it takes to span that distance. And because the primary objects that a hunter will be trying to use for ranging are most likely to be game animals, it would be good to know the numbers that go along with them.

Although the following are simply averages and will vary, they are close enough to be of some value in determining range. These are the heights in inches from the bottom of the brisket to the top of the withers for the animals listed (if measuring from the top of the back instead of the withers, a few inches, such as 2 inches for a whitetail, may be deducted):

Whitetailed Deer: 18 inches[vii]
Elk: 24 inches
Sheep: 22½ inches
Black Bear: 18 inches[viii]
Pronghorn Antelope: 14 inches
Coyote: 9 inches
Rockchuck (standing, i.e., measure from head to foot): 18 inches
Prairie Dog (standing): 9 inches

There is a formula for calculating yardage based on the number of mils subtending the target animal:

(Target Height in Yards X 1,000) ÷ Target Height in Mils = Range in Yards

Using the example of the whitetail again (with its body width of 18 inches equaling 0.5 yards), if its body width were subtended by 1.25 mils the range would be calculated:

(0.5 Yards X 1,000) ÷ 1.25 Mils = 400 yards

At this point a hunter needs to know what the bullet drop is for the cartridge and load he is using. A 165-grain .30-caliber bullet fired from a factory-loaded .30-'06 cartridge at a muzzle velocity of 2,800 feet per second will drop 29½ inches at 400 yards. To "compensate" for the drop, another calculation can be made:

Target Distance in Yards ÷ 100 = Value in Inches per MOA

So to raise the point of aim in this particular scenario, as-suming that the riflescope has been sighted in at zero height at 100 yards, the hunter would calculate:

400 Yards ÷ 100 = 4 Inches per MOA

In other words each MOA of adjustment made to the point of aim in the scope would change the point of impact by 4 inches, meaning that a hunter would have to raise the elevation of his point of aim by about 7½ MOA in this ex-ample with the .30-'06. For a scope with ¼ MOA adjust-ments, that would mean 29½ clicks (one click for 1 inch of compensation with a ¼ MOA scope will, alas, work only at exactly 400 yards).

The very large assumption is that a hunter will have the time to figure this all out. Compensation charts can be pre-pared, of course, and some hunters actually tape them to the stocks of their rifles, like a singer-songwriter taping his songlist for the night's gig to the back of his Gibson twelve-string. Besides mil dots, some scopes come with mechanical range estimators that use the *stadia* wire (the fine portion of a duplex reticle) as a fixed measurement. Usually the distance from the back, rather than the withers, of a white-tail to the brisket (16 inches) will correspond to the dis-tance subtended by the stadia from the center of the crosshair to the *picket* (the top point of the lower heavy post) at 200 yards. The deer will fill less of this gap the far-ther away it gets. If the power selector ring also has a yardage-estimating scale, the hunter can find the range by turning the ring, increasing the magnification, until the width of the deer's body again fits between the crosshair and the picket. He then has only to look at the yardage number shown on the ring to find the range. Even without this scale, the stadia should be a known subtension at a particular yardage and should be shown in the riflescope's technical data. In the long run a hunter is more likely to use mil dots or range-estimating scales or even stadia length to give him a fair guess at distances rather than as the basis for mathematical equations.

- The **rings** hold the riflescope to the **bases,** and the bases hold the rings and scope to the rifle, and so they are known as a group as "scope mounts." The ins and outs of mounting the various types of bases to a rifle (or shotgun or muzzle-loader) and the rings to the bases are best explained by reading the mounting instructions that come with the scope mounts. A hunter should look for the mounts that best match his rifle based on several questions: Are they strong enough for magnum recoil?; are they trim enough not to add unnecessary ounces to an ultra-lightweight mountain rifle?; are they "quick detachable"?; do they match or complement the finish of the scope?; and so on. The mounts should also be as low as possible—*stay low to stay steady*—but leave the bolt handle or other parts of the action with enough room to be worked properly. The scope should contact only the rings and no part of the firearm.

  With the bases fully tightened by their screws (a dab of low-strength Loctite on the threads of the screws will help keep the bases in place while still allowing the hunter to re-move them with relative ease at some future date if he wishes) and the scope set in the rings, the hunter can then snug up the screws in the rings, using equal pressure all around until the scope can just barely be moved in the rings. Pushing the scope as far forward as it will go in the mounts, the hunter brings the *unloaded rifle* up to his shoulder and draws back the scope until he can just see the full field of view in the eyepiece. He can also do this while wearing heavy or light hunting clothes and while taking different shooting positions—sitting, kneeling, prone, up, down—depending on what hunting condition he expects to encounter. A hunter wants to find that sweet spot that will give him the largest possible eye box (as described earlier, this is the range of distance at which the ocular can be held from the sighting eye and still provide a full field of view) while leaving enough space between the bell of the scope and his eye to avoid severe laceration of his brow when the rifle recoils (known colloquially as the "mark of the Weatherby" by the less charitable). If he can hold the rifle securely in something like a gun vise, he can then turn the scope until he is sure that the vertical crosshair is exactly perpendicular to the line of the bore (and there are several tools available for doing this). Being a little off is not a cause for serious alarm, but it's *just not right!* Too much, though, *can* bring about an aiming problem.

The various screws involved in mounting a riflescope's bases and rings have recommended amounts of torque that should be applied to them for proper hold. A torque driver or wrench will be needed to get these exactly right:

Base Screws: 30 inch-pounds
Windage Screws (if any—*see "Plainsman" earlier*):
   30–40 inch-pounds
Ring Screws (aluminum rings): 10–15 inch-pounds
Ring Screws (steel rings): 15–20 inch-pounds
Rifle Stocks (without pillar bedding): 40 inch-pounds
Rifle Stocks (with pillar bedding): up to 65 inch-pounds

The screws in the stock are known as the *action screws* (they hold the barreled action in the stock). Most rifles will have two—a front and a rear—in the bottom of the stock. Some stocks have a third, middle one, which should be only slightly tightened. Because that middle screw seems to serve no function that has ever truly been explained to anyone's satisfaction, no one knows what it is doing in the stock. Its existence has seen the best firearms' minds of many a generation destroyed by madness.

In any case, with all the screws correctly tightened (Loctite is not necessary on the ring screws), the hunter can now sight in the scope. It is easiest to begin with a *bore-sighting collimator* (another optical device that aligns the bore with the point of aim of the riflescope). This should get the scope onto the target at the shooting range. There the hunter should start out firing at 25 yards, and if he is not able to hit the target, he should get closer, if possible, or use a bigger target. If the hunter has not had the benefit of a collimator, he can "bore sight" the rifle at the range by placing it in a solid rest, removing the bolt, looking through the bore *from the breech*, and positioning the rifle until the target's bull's-eye is visible in the center of the bore. Then, without moving the rifle, he turns the windage and elevation adjustments until the reticle is aligned with the bull's-eye, turning them in the opposite directions from those indicated on the knobs. In bore-sighting in this way, the directions are reversed, as they are when adjusting the front sight on a rifle with iron sights—up for down, etc.

Once the hunter has the rifle grouping consistently at 25 yards, he can move the target out to 100 yards. Too often hunters use a rolled-up blanket or, worse, a hard metal or plastic box as a rest when sighting in, or they will even rest the rifle on the *barrel* rather than on the stock. In order to accurately sight in a rifle at all, a good rest is called for, one that is made specifically for target shooting. Such a rest can be found in any of the better gunshops or outdoor-product catalogs. Accuracy when sighting in also depends on the rifle's resting on the same portion of the stock, usually closer to the floorplate than to the fore-end, for each shot.

With a solid rest and a scope that is already "on the paper," a hunter can zero in a rifle at 100 yards with two shots. Aiming at the center of the target, the hunter will fire one shot. Wherever the shot hits, the hunter, with the rifle held firmly in the rest or vise, will place the scope's crosshair on the bull's-eye again and without moving the rifle will adjust windage and elevation until the crosshair is centered on the first bullet hole. The second shot should then strike the bull's-eye. A tight three-shot group from a "cold" barrel will verify that the rifle is striking where it is being aimed or indicate that further adjustment is needed. With the rifle sighted in, a hunter can protect the lenses from dust and moisture with a good scope cover.

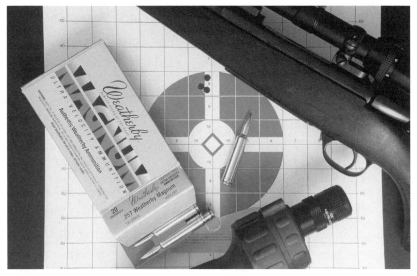

The ideal "zero" for a riflescope on a hunting rifle—2½-inches high at 100 yards.

Riflescopes were in wide use by the time of the Civil War. Photo courtesy of Picture Collection, The Branch Libraries, The New York Public Library, Astor, Lenox and Tilden Foundations.

A young sheep-hunting guide once told his client that the way he got along with folks in the wilds of Alaska was never to discuss with them religion, politics, or ballistics, which is another way of saying that everybody has a different opinion about where a riflescope should be zeroed in. Some say that a zero setting at 100 yards is adequate; while many an East Coast hunter, faced with the prospect of hunting in wide-open spaces of the West, has taken the very silly step of sighting in 6 or 8 inches high, assuming that the game out there is never shot at ranges of less than a quarter-mile. All things considered, the former is much preferable to the latter; but for most hunting situations, sighting in 2 to 2½ inches high at 100 yards will give a hunter the greatest flexibility in the field—if that is not too controversial a position to take.

SIDELIGHT:

The most spectacular shot made by a sharpshooter during the Civil War was fired from the Confederate lines. In 1862 the Confederate Congress authorized the forming of a sharpshooter unit. While their Union counterparts carried Sharpses and heavy target rifles, the Confederates were armed with the truly elegant .50-caliber British Whitworth rifle.

On May 9 of 1864, at the Battle of Spotsylvania Courthouse in Virginia, Union Major General John Sedgwick, grandson of one of Washington's generals, was leading his VI Corps of the Army of the Potomac. Sedgwick, an artillery officer and West Point graduate, had seen combat during the Seminole and Mexican-American Wars, the Utah War against an uprising of Mormons, and against Indians in Kansas. During the three years of the Civil War, Sedgwick received wounds in the arm and leg at the Battle of Glendale and wounds to the wrist, leg, and shoulder at Antietam when his division was attacked on three sides by the forces under Major General "Stonewall" Jackson.

At Spotsylvania Courthouse, Sedgwick was directing the placement of cannons and was warned by one of his staff not to appear in the open at a particular position because every officer who had gone there that day had been hit. Sedgwick agreed to stay clear, but later his subordinate and he forgot about the danger and went to the emplacement. When a sharpshooter's bullet whizzed past, and some of Sedgwick's men flinched and ducked, he chided them with a laugh, "What! What! Men, dodging this way for single bullets! What will you do when they open fire along the whole line? I am ashamed of you. They couldn't hit an elephant at this distance." A few moments later another bullet flew by, and a soldier near Sedgwick threw himself onto the ground.

"Why, my man," Sedgwick said, nudging him with the toe of his boot, "I'm ashamed of you, dodging that way." And once more he said, "They couldn't hit an elephant at this distance." The soldier got up, saluted, and said, "General, I dodged a shell once, and if I hadn't, it would have taken my head off. I believe in dodging." Sedgwick laughed and said, "All right, man; go to your place."

As Sedgwick was smiling over the encounter and watching the man go off, 800 to 1,000 yards away, Sergeant E. R. Grace of the Fourth Georgia Infantry was taking aim with his Whitworth. Another shot whistled in and ended with a thudding sound. As Sedgwick's subordinate started to speak to him, the general turned with blood spurting from his cheek below his left eye and fell dead. Sedgwick was the highest-ranking Union officer to be killed during the war. His death delayed an attack against General Robert E. Lee, resulting in Lee's winning the battle.

OTHER OPTICS 6

Viewing things is not the only purpose of optics for the hunter. In the broadest sense of the word, optics can also apply to devices that create images, measure distances, and illuminate the hunter's path.

The images created by hunting optics fall under the broad rubric of *red-dot* sights. Other names for these types of aiming devices are "reflex" or "infinity" sights. These sights use reflective or refractive optics to create a luminous or reflective reticle that can be collimated with the bore of the firearm. The reticle appears to be located out at infinity, although no light is actually projected forward from the device. The advantages of these sights are their unbearable, or rather extremely bearable lightness (as little as 3 or 4 ounces), essentially unlimited eye relief, a significant absence of parallax, swift target acquisition, and, because they generally lack any magnification (1X is usual, though some sights are 2X), the allowance they give a hunter to shoot with both eyes open. These advantages make all the red-dot scopes especially suitable for handguns and shotguns and perhaps less so for high-powered rifles for which higher magnification may be desirable.

Some of the first red-dot sights used fiber-optics material to illuminate a reticle passively by collecting ambient light. A hunter did not look through the sight but rather *into* it with one eye; with both eyes open as he sighted, his brain would superimpose the reticle onto the target. These types of sights were known as *occluded*.

Most red-dot sights today can be looked *through* with a single eye, although they still work better when the hunter sights with both eyes and allows the brain to superimpose the reticle onto the target. Red dots may come in a tube design similar to a standard riflescope, or they may simply be a flat base with a frame for holding the reflective surface onto which the reticle is projected.

The source of a projected reticle is usually a red *LED,* or "light-emitting diode." The light is reflected off the rear of the objective lens and back to the ocular, along with all the other light entering the sight (the absence of most of a regular scope's glass, such as the erector, being the reason for the red dot's low weight). The intensity of the brightness of the reticle is controlled by a rheostat and adjusted by a graduated dial so that on a bright day it can be turned all the way up to "11," just like Nigel Tufnel's amp, except that many red dots even go to "13" for reasons known fully only to the manufacturers. The size of the reticle can vary from 2 MOA to 4 MOA, depending on which size a hunter chooses in anticipation of the size and speed of the quarry; and there can be instances when a hunter might want an even larger reticle. In Scandinavia, for instance, red dots are popular among hunters who organize drives to push deer and elk (i.e., what an American hunter would recognize as a red stag and a moose) out of the forest, the game moving at a fair pace as it breaks from the trees. A bigger red dot could make for faster tracking and aiming.

The newest type of red dot is a holographic sight that uses lasers to project the reticle image. This sight, similar in principle to the "heads up" display that a jet-fighter pilot sees on the inside of the canopy of his cockpit, offers the hunter a variety of crosshairs at the turn of a dial, from a 1-MOA dot to large and small circles, dual circles, diamond, and even tombstone shapes.

When hunting with a red-dot sight, there is seemingly scant call for this next piece of optics, the *rangefinder*. At 1X bullet drop isn't much of a concern, so determining the precise distance to the target is a bit of literal overkill. When the range begins to stretch out past 200 or 300 yards, though, then knowing the distance to within a narrow degree of certainty can indeed be critical. Using a riflescope's reticle to determine distance has already been dis-

A present-day laser rangefinder.

cussed; with only the stadia to use as a measuring device, though, it is more a matter of range estimating than range finding.

The concept of the rangefinder is a very old one, with its origins, not surprisingly, in military history. Gunners needed to know the distances to their targets, and they couldn't run out from the emplacements and take the measurement across the battlefield in a series of chains. So the science of *trigonometry* was called upon. By *triangulation,* the angles and distances to a particular point could be arrived at. To determine these angles, measuring devices were employed, the most famous one and the one used from the late sixteenth century into the nineteenth century being the *graphometer*. The graphometer consisted of a brass graduated semicircle with two *alidades*—flat strips with sights that revolve around the radius of the semicircle, the name meaning "sighting rods" and derived from the Arab word *al-'iḍāda*.

The graphometer was developed by Philippe Danfrie. He was superintendent of the Paris mint and engraved French coins and medals and designed and made typefaces as well as scientific instruments. Using one of his own typefaces, he published *Déclaration et l'Usage du Graphomètre, par la pratique duquel l'on peut mesurer toutes distances des choses de remarque qui se pourront voir et discerner du lieu où il sera posé: et pour arpenter terres, bois, prez et faire plans de villes forteresses, cartes géographiques et généralement toutes mesures visibles: et ce sans reigle d'Arithmétique* ("Declaration on the Use of the Graphometer. . . etc." Danfrie's 34-page treatise on the graphometer in its first 1597 printing is today worth about $16,500.)

The graphometer was not an optical instrument only to the degree to which it did not have lenses, unless the lens covering the compass that was usually a part of the device counts. Optical rangefinders, known as *coincidence rangefinders* (or *CRF*), came into use in the early nineteenth century. In a CRF two images of the same target, seen at different angles, would be brought

An early Zeiss "coincidence rangefinder." Photo courtesy of
Carl Zeiss, Inc.

together by the viewer until they overlapped in the field of view,
and the distance recorded by the device could then be read. The
two image viewers on these CRFs could be anywhere from 3 to
dozens of feet apart, depending on how accurate the measurements had to be.

Zeiss would eventually develop a CRF small enough to be
held in the hand, but credit for the very first "short-base" CRF
must go to a pair of professors at Yorkshire College in Leeds,
England, now the University of Leeds. In 1888 Archibald Barr,
an engineering professor, and William Stroud, a professor of
physics, entered a competition held by the British War Office to
design a CRF that an infantryman could carry. The CRF they
submitted was unacceptable to the Army; but Barr and Stroud
produced a modified and improved version that was sent on sea

trials by the Admiralty, which was impressed enough to offer them a contract for six of the instruments in 1892. Dubbed the "NRF No. 1" Barr and Stroud's CRF was eventually accepted for the entire Royal Navy, and by the start of World War I every British battleship and battlecruiser had at least nine of the devices on board, and the CRFs had found their way onto the ships of navies of Japan, Italy, and France and, in a redesigned instrument, into the armies of Great Britain, the Austro-Hungarian Empire, and France.

CRFs, at least the kinds that hunters are likely to carry, can work very well but as a rule are at their best at shorter ranges, such as those that an archery or muzzleloader hunter might encounter. In using a CRF, a hunter will want to take various distance readings of visible landmarks at different ranges before the appearance of an animal. He should look for a strong vertical line, such as a single sapling, take several readings, then calculate the average distance. In this way, if an animal does come into view, a hunter will know that when it is beside that aspen tree or that red rock, it is so many yards away.

Trying to range an animal with either a CRF or a laser rangefinder is no easy chore. In reality, ranging an animal is probably easier with a CRF than with a laser rangefinder because an animal is not very reflective; but in either case it is better to find the distances to assorted landmarks where an animal might appear or position itself. The preceding assumes that a hunter is doing his rangefinding by himself, while in a Panglossian world he would have another hunter or guide assisting him with the ranging duties, supplying him with a steady stream of yardages as an animal moved nearer or farther.

With a laser rangefinder it may be even more important to have fixed, reflective targets to take distance measurements on. A *laser rangefinder* uses a laser beam and a really, really accurate timer to calculate distances. The laser is pulsed at a "hard" or reflective target—a flat rock or the side of an old shed, for example—and the time (sub-nanoseconds) that it takes the beam to bounce back to the finder is calculated against the speed of light, thus determining the distance. Laser rangefinding is far from foolproof. The beam may be reflected off intervening leaves or brush or refracted by heat shimmer and is not usually very accurate beyond 1,000 yards or in extremely open terrain. But where a CRF might be able to find ranges of 100 yards, a laser rangefinder can measure distances of 500 and 600 yards (about the maximum range at which any rifle hunter, and in reality only the best, should consider taking a shot) with a high degree of precision.

As with the CRF, as discussed earlier, the laser rangefinder should be used to premeasure distances; and as with the CRF as well, the distances should be based on the averages of several readings. The first handheld laser rangefinder was built by Leica in 1993 for surveying and construction work. As far as is known, all it did was measure distances. Today laser rangefinders for hunters can measure the degree of incline or decline of a slope to determine the actual ballistics range for both rifles and bows, show MOA adjustments for particular cartridge loads, indicate holdover points for aiming, see through leaves, brush, and rain, and even tell the hunter how wide the spread is on the buck he is viewing. As has been said, though, "One man's justice is another's injustice; one man's beauty another's ugliness; one man's wisdom another's folly." There are only so many slices of cold cuts you can, or would want, to stack in a sandwich; and maybe a rangefinder that simply finds ranges reliably ought to be good enough.

For most of human existence nearly all artificial light (a peculiar term because of the vague insinuation of fraudulence—how can light not be light?—though, of course, the word refers merely to the manmade origins, the handcrafting of that light) was the product of incandescence. Campfires, torches, candles, reflecting lanterns all illuminated through the release of thermal radiation in the visible form of light: It burned, it glowed, it gave off light.

The footlights in nineteenth-century theaters were chunks of calcium oxide heated white hot by torches. This chemical compound had an extremely high melting point and gave off a very satisfactory glow. It was derived by heating limestone in a kiln, which led to the phrase, if not the entire notion, of being "in the limelight." Gas lanterns work in a somewhat similar fashion, with a mantle substituted for a block of burnt lime.

A gas-lantern mantle is a silk pouch that has been impregnated with an oxide or mixture of oxides. Most hunters are familiar with the ritual of installing a new mantle and then burning it off. What appears to be left behind is an ashy residue, like a skeleton of the mantle. In fact, this is a ceramic-mesh cage or envelope produced by the oxide material's being heated as the silk was flamed away, which when heated again itself by burning gas will glow white hot.

Even electric light is a form of incandescence, with the heat created by the resistance of the filament to the passage of electricity through it. Thomas Edison was by no means the discoverer of electric incandescent light, by the way. The true origins of the electric light go back at least as far as Count Alessandro Giuseppe Antonio Anastasio Volta. Born in Como, Lombardy, in 1745, Volta was a slow learner, being unable to speak until age four. His parents later handed him to the Jesuits, hoping he would become a jurist, but Volta turned to physics instead. In 1800 he produced the first wet-cell electric battery out of sulfuric acid, copper, and zinc, the copper being the positive pole, and the zinc the negative. In 1881 in honor of his achievements Volta's name was given to the unit of electricity named, of couse, the "volt."

In 1802 Sir Humphry Davy, a professor at the Royal Institution of Great Britain, where one of his later students would be the great English chemist and physicist Michael Faraday, used a more powerful version of Volta's battery (in fact, the world's most powerful at the time) to create the first electric incandescent light by passing a current through a thin strip of platinum. The value of this was mostly experimental, and Davy's most famous invention, the "Davy lamp," was a candle lamp that could be safely used by coal miners in deep shafts in the presence of combustible gases.

The first light bulb appeared in 1840 when the British scientist Warren de la Rue combined a platinum filament, chosen because of its high melting point, with a vacuum tube. This device's only real failing was the platinum's lack of cost efficiency. Many other efforts followed. Historians list twenty-two inventors of the electric light bulb before two men, working separately, arrived at the first practical and commercial versions.

One man was the English physicist and chemist Joseph Wilson Swan, whose earliest attempts at a light bulb dated back to 1860. In 1878 he received a British patent for his device based on a carbon filament and an improved vacuum inside the bulb and began installing light bulbs in homes.

In the same year in New Jersey, the "Wizard of Menlo Park," Thomas Alva Edison, having shrewdly paid two Canadian medical electricians $5,000 for the patent rights to their promising approach to light-bulb making, filed his own U.S. patent application for an "Improvement in Electric Lights." He told the press that he had successfully tested his carbon-filament light bulb, hoping the publicity from this would attract grant money. The truth is that Edison's first test of his light bulb did not come until October 22, 1879, his bulb emitting light continuously for nearly fourteen hours. Within a few months Edison and his staff would discover filaments capable of lasting almost one hundred times as long. It is because of these filaments, higher vacuums in the bulbs, greater resistance in the lamps that permitted the use of power from an industrially viable central source, and, not least, the development of an entire system for electrification of towns and cities that Edison deserves the title of "Inventor of the Electric Light."

In 1888 a German scientist, Dr. Carl Gassner, made the acid-filled wet-cell batteries of the time practicable and safe by enclosing their chemicals and components in a zinc casing. Now batteries could be truly portable, so, of course, their first application was in novelty items. The roots of the flashlight are said to go back to 1896 and Joshua Lionel Cowen. Born "Joshua Lionel Cohen" in 1877, he was the eighth of nine children of Jewish immigrants. A college dropout, Cowen came up with a flowerpot illuminated with battery-powered lights. It was less than a commercial success, and Cowen sold his company to a Russian émigré, Akiba Horowitz, and went on to start another company that made model trains, calling it by his middle name, the Lionel Corporation.[ix]

Horowitz, born in Minsk in 1856, changed his name to "Conrad Hubert" in 1891 and started the American Electrical Novelty & Manufacturing Company. By 1896 only a few, relatively small "D-cell" batteries were required to produce light. In that year the Birdsall Electric company, a maker of battery devices, went broke, and one of Birdsall's employees, David Misell, went to work for Hubert, patenting several battery-powered lights for him, including the tubular "flashlight." The name was based on the batteries' inability to hold a charge for a sustained period of time, causing the light to dim and the device to be switched off until the power could once more build up. Hubert and Misell gave several of these devices to some of New York's finest, who offered favorable testimonials in return. Within a few years Hubert had an entire line of flashlights, which he marketed under the brand name of "Ever Ready."

A *flashlight* to this day remains that tube that Misell designed to hold batteries and a parabolic mirror to reflect the light emitted by a small incandescent bulb. The first real advancement in this design was the introduction of the *halogen* light bulb. A halogen light uses a tungsten filament encased in a small quartz envelope inside the lamp or bulb. This envelope is filled with either iodine or bromide gas, both of which are members of the halogen, or "salt-former," family of five nonmetallic elements. This arrangement of tungsten and halogen gas allows the filament to burn both hotter and brighter; and as it evaporates and gives off tungsten atoms, those atoms combine with the gas and are deposited back on the filament, giving it a longer life.

The truly great breakthrough in flashlight technology was the invention of the light-emitting diode. This is the first device suitable for a flashlight that does not produce light through incandescence. The first known LED dates back to 1907, but no one then was able to discern a practical application for it. A practical LED was invented by Nick Holonyak Jr. in 1962 while he was working for General Electric. And the first one was red.

While an incandescent bulb might be thought of as the Edison light, the LED is more like the Einstein light, in which a semiconductor chip directly produces quanta of electromagnetic energy in the form of light photons and in true colors. This probably makes sense only to someone currently enrolled at MIT.

There isn't really an easy way to explain how an LED works except to say that its light comes from *electroluminescence*. Unlike incandescence, whose light is a byproduct of heat, electroluminescence is the result of the recombination of electrons and holes in a material such as a semiconductor. The "excited" electrons in the material give off their energy in the form of photons, i.e., light.

The advantages of the LED over the incandescent bulb are more light per watt, a plus for battery power, "pure" colored light without the use of filters, compact size, solid-state components that can withstand greater external shock, extremely long life, and when LEDs burn out they dim over time instead of flaring out without warning.

The red and blue lights of an LED, along with white, are very useful to a hunter trying to find his way to his treestand or elsewhere in the dark. Turning the flashlight to red lets a hunter see the ground without losing his night vision and without being detected by game. Red and blue lights, and especially a combination of the two, are excellent, as well, for finding blood signs in the dark when a hunter is on the trail of a wounded animal. In the dark, under a combination of red-blue LED lights, fresh blood drops will stand out as black, and the absence of visible white light is less likely to spook a wounded animal into getting up and running on.

Before buying a flashlight, in particular a more expensive one—and some LED models machined from titanium can cost upward of $300—a hunter wants to look at the beam projected on a solid-colored wall in a dark room. The "hot spot" in the center of the beam should be intense, and fall away in a uniformly diminishing corona that is without rings, rays, or spots. Such aberrations are nothing less than holes in light in which objects and animals can be hidden.

Some flashlight manufacturers try to pitch the "adjustable focus" of the beams on their products as a plus. In reality it means a manufacturer is incapable of building a flashlight that is properly focused to begin with. There is only one optimum setting for the light source in a flashlight in relation to the reflector. If the manufacturer has not adjusted the light source in the flashlight to that setting in his factory, and is expecting a hunter to remedy the situation, he is selling an inferior product that will never provide the intensity and quality of light that a hunter ought to expect.

The options for carrying a flashlight in the field include holding it in the hand, attaching it to the clothing, or wearing it

LED headlamp, left, and LED handheld flashlight, right.

on the head. Attaching it to clothing, though a hands-free method, will tend to cause the light to wobble around. A headlamp is also hands free, allowing a hunter to point the beam in the exact direction into which he wants to look. Wearing a headlamp, though, usually eliminates the ability to wear a hat or cap, and the weight and pressue it exerts on the forehead can become uncomfortable after a certain amount of time. A handheld light offers the most versatility and accuracy, but there is always the prospect of setting it down and walking away from it. A lanyard or a retractable cable "keeper," like keys that are hung from a belt, are good ways to avoid cursing the darkness.

SIDELIGHT:

For thousands of years light was believed to be a "presence" with immeasurable speed. This belief arose from the concept of Aristotle and others that vision is the product of rays emitted by the eyes. When the eyes are opened, distant objects such as stars are immediately visible. Galileo, as was his wont, harshly mocked the Aristotelians' position in *Dialogue on the Two Great World Systems*. Yet, genuine proponents of the scientific method, such as Kepler, the Elizabethan Sir Francis Bacon (reputed resorter to catamites and said to have died from pneumonia contracted from the carcass of a chicken upon which he was experimenting with the use of snow to preserve meat), and the French mathematician René Descartes (who died while tutoring Queen Christina in Protestant Sweden and as a Catholic was interred in a cemetery reserved for unbaptized infants), explained the seeming instantaneity of light by hypothesizing that its speed is infinite. Before them, of course, Alhazen had stated that vision is the result of light emitted from a source and reflected into the eye at a finite speed.

Galileo did attempt to take a physical measurement of the speed of light, his experiment a modification of that for measuring the speed of sound. He placed an assistant with a lantern on a distant hill and himself with a lantern on another. The lanterns were closed, and the assistant was instructed to unshade his at the exact moment he detected light from Galileo's. It proved impossible to calculate an elapsed time that could not be attributed to the reaction time between the two experimenters, leading Galileo to conclude that light travels at a very, very great rate of speed.

In 1676 Danish astronomer Ole Rømer in his study of the Jovian moon Io noted a discrepancy in the predicted time of its eclipse by Jupiter, which he ascribed to the variation in the distance of Io from the Earth at different periods in their orbits. His work led Newton to conclude that it takes light some eight minutes to travel from the sun to the Earth, although that did not provide a velocity, the distance from the Earth to the sun being unknown.

For the eighteenth-century English astronomer James Bradley, starlight reminded him of rain falling steadily straight down onto the Earth. If someone walks into the rain, it appears to have a slight slant, based on the speed of the walker. Starlight, too, should have something of this same property because of the movement of the Earth through space. Bradley deduced that starlight exhibits just such an "aberration" and used this to compute a speed of light of 298,000 kilometers per second.

Researchers continued to seek an empirical rather than deductive determination of light speed; and in the mid-1800s two competing French physicists, Armand-Hippolyte Louis Fizeau and Jean Bernard Léon Foucault, devised similar instruments involving mirrors and rotating wheels (Foucault also made a pendulum to demonstrate the Earth's rotation, this device destined to become the title of an Umberto Eco novel, *Il pendolo di Foucault*). Fizeau's results were too high, while Foucault's were close to Bradley's deduction and near the actual figure.

That figure was discovered by the American Albert Abraham Michelson. Born in Strzelno, Poland, in 1852 he was raised in Murphy's Camp, California, and Virginia City, Nevada, to where his merchant father Samuel emigrated from Poland before Albert was four. A Jew, Michelson received from Ulysses S. Grant a rare appointment to Annapolis as a naval midshipman in 1869. In 1878, now married and a physics and chemistry instructor at the U.S. Naval Academy, he used Foucault's mirrors-and-wheels method—the dimensions of the experiment lengthened from 60 feet to 2,000, measured to within 1/10th of an inch—to fix the speed of light at 186,355 miles per second, plus or minus 30 miles per second, more accurate than Foucault's results by a factor of 20 and close enough for government work. He later refined this figure to 186,285 miles (or 299,796 kilometers) per second. Today the speed of light is set *by definition,* adopted in 1983 at the seventeenth *Conférence Générale des Poids et Mesures,* at

299,792,458 meters (186,282.397 miles) per second, based on the frequency of microwaves. This is the value of c in Albert Einstein's famous equation $e=mc^2$.

Michelson's greatest contribution to physics, though, may be the result of his experiment in 1887 with Edward Williams Morley at what is now Case Western Reserve University in Cleveland, Ohio, an experiment that failed to achieve its desired result. At the time it was believed that space and all vacuums are filled with a medium known as "luminiferous aether." As sound needs air to travel within and through, it was held that light needs a similar medium and that this medium is the aether. Michelson and Morley created an experimental apparatus known as a "interferometer," placed on a large block of marble and floated in a pool of mercury to dampen all possible vibrations, and used it to measure the shift in the amount of interference fringes between the two halves of a split beam of light. The fact that no significant degree of fringing could be detected led the two scientists to the conclusion that the existence of the aether could not be proved. This is considered one of the most important examples in science in which being wrong was right, and this work was a major factor in Michelson's winning of the Nobel Prize in physics in 1907, becoming the first American to be given a scientific Nobel.

Michelson's honors did not end with that, of course. Even long after his death he continued to accumulate accolades. One of the most famous is the 1962 episode of *Bonanza,* "Look to the Stars," in which Ben Cartwright defends a fictionalized teenaged Michelson against the narrow-minded anti-Semitism of post-Civil War Virginia City and in which Michelson tries to replicate Foucault's experiment on the dusty street outside the Silver Dollar.

AFTERWORD

As was written in the introduction to this book, its object is not so much to teach hunters how better to purchase optics as to provide them with a deeper understanding of the history and construction of hunting optics, and the most useful application of them in the field.

Ortega y Gasset said that the one thing a hunter must "essentially do," ahead of hiking, stalking, and shooting well is "the least muscular of all operations: looking." Advances in optical technology do nothing to alter the fundamentals of that essential activity. Hunters remain bound to the basic, invariable physical laws and mechanics governing vision and optics. No assembly of glass lenses can ever substitute for a hunter's eyes and brain. Good optics, though, can enhance his looking to a very considerable degree.

Good optics are, by so many definitions, a tribute to man's continually "seeing the light." While the hunter must always be looking with his eyes, it is his optics that can bring the view into sharper focus. The optics a hunter uses can be marvelous devices. He should always remember, though, that those optics were not meant to see with, but to see *through*. What matters most in the hunt is what lies on either side of the glass.

NOTES

i   Shooting glasses afford progressively less protection as shot size increases and as distance from the gun decreases.

ii   Glasses worn on the trap-and-skeet range often need to be set higher on the face to center the lenses on the targets in flight.

iii   Unfortunately, there's one more comparative number to look at, and that is *relative brightness*. This number is determined by squaring the exit pupil (e.g., an exit pupil of 4 millimeters would work out to a relative brightness of 4^2 or 16. A relative brightness of 25, the square of a 5-millimeter exit pupil, is considered the optimum in all light conditions; but again for present-day optics, this and twilight factor are of real value only as comparisons between optics with lenses and antireflectivity of equally top quality.

iv   In this case, though, there is still the pesky problem of a relative brightness of 25 for the binocular and a mere 1.77 for the spotting scope.

v   Before the Porro-prism slips beneath the waves, it would still be good to have a mnemonic to help straighten out which is which: Is the bent binocular a "roof" or a "Porro"? The versatile outdoor writer and optics expert John Barsness came up with as reliable an *aide-mémoire* as any. He advised thinking of the bend in the Porro-prism binocular as a dogleg and simply saying, "Ah, poor old dogleg!"

vi   In the same year a $1,000 prize was offered to the winner of an hour-long race on a 1-mile running track in Hoboken, New Jersey. Thirty thousand spectators attended, some breaking down fences to gain entry. Runners from Britain, and even several Native Americans, were in the field. With less than three minutes to go an Englishman led, but American John Gildersleeve overtook him and went on to win with a total distance of 10 miles and 955 yards. The prize would be worth more than $26,000 in today's money for an hour's work.

vii   A mule deer may be slightly larger.

viii This is very arbitrary. It is extremely difficult to see the line of a bear's brisket, down in the grass and weeds somewhere, and bears can vary tremendously in size.

ix Retiring in 1959, Cowen sold his fifty-five thousand shares of Lionel stock to his great-nephew, Roy Cohn, famous for, among other things, being one of Senator Joseph McCarthy's aides during the infamous Army-McCarthy hearings in 1954.

INDEX

instinctive shooting, 2–3

*Instructions to Young Marksmen,
in All that Relates to the
General Construction,
Practical Manipulation,
Causes and Liability to Error
in Making Accurate Rifle
Performances, and the
Theoretic Principles upon
Which Such Accurate
Performances Are Founded,
as Exhibited in the Improved
American Rifle* (Chapman),
106–7

interpupillary distance (IPD), 70

J

Jackson, Stonewall, 127–28

James, Morgan, 107

Janssen, Zacharias, 32

K

Kahles, Karl Robert, 99

Kajiwara, Kumao, 63

Kalbach, Ed, 27–28

Kellner, Carl, 61

Kepler, Johannes, 14, 33–34, 142

*Kitab-al-Manadhirn, the Book of
Optics* (Ibn al-Haitham), 14

Kuhn-Leitz, Elsie, 62

L

Lee, Robert E., 128

Leitz, Ernst, 61–62

Leitz, Ernst II, 62

Leitz Freedom Train, 62

lenses
achromatic, 34–35
antireflective coatings, 36–37, 69
apochromatic, 35, 57
chromatic aberration, 34–35,
36, 79
cleaning, 26–28, 91–92
concave, 16–17, 33
convex, 17, 33
curvature, 20
eight-base curve, 20
elements, 35
groups, 35
magnifying, 25
materials, 19–20
plano, 20–21, 23, 24, 25
reduction of aberration, 35
reflection, 36–37
spherical aberration, 35, 42
Visby, 32
wraparounds, 20, 21, 23, 24–25

lens pens, 26, 92

Leupold, Markus Frederich
"Fred," 111–12

Leupold, Norbert and
Marcus, 112

Leupold & Stevens, 112

light
artificial, 135–41
incandescent, 136–38, 139
speed of, 141–44

light-emitting diodes (LED), 130,
139–40

linear magnification, 30